Outwitting Toddlers

Outwitting Toddlers

and Other Small Human Beings

Real Advice from Real Parents

Edited by Bill Adler, Jr.,
and Peggy Robin

Illustrations by Loel Barr

Lowell House
Los Angeles

Contemporary Books
Chicago

Library of Congress Cataloging-in-Publication Data

Outwitting toddlers: and newborns, infants, tots, little children, and other small human beings: a compendium of real advice from real parents / edited by Bill Adler, Jr., and Peggy Robin.
   p. cm.
ISBN 1-56565-032-8
1. Parenting—Handbooks, manuals, etc. 2. Child rearing—Handbooks, manuals, etc. 3. Infants—Care—Handbooks, manuals, etc. 4. Children—Care—Handbooks, manuals, etc. I. Adler, Bill. II. Robin, Peggy.
HQ772.098   1993
649'. 1 — dc20   92-34020
                                                                CIP

Lowell House
2029 Century Park East, Suite 3290
Los Angeles, CA 90067

Publisher: Jack Artenstein
Vice-President/Editor-in-Chief: Janice Gallagher
Director of Publishing Services: Mary D. Aarons
Text Design: Judy Doud Lewis

Manufactured in the United States of America
10 9 8 7 6 5 4 3 2 1

To the grandparents

Contents

Contents

Acknowledgments

Our greatest thanks go to Mary Ellen Koenig, whose efforts as senior researcher for this book were invaluable.

Gracious thanks are extended to all the parents who took the time to relate their experiences to us. They truly made this a book for parents *by parents*.

Thanks to Janice Gallagher, who kept this project going. Beth Pratt-Dewey, as always, contributed to making this a success.

Finally, Betsy Amster had the insight to know a good book idea when it pounced on her desk. Thanks, Betsy!

Introduction

Who gives the best advice about babies? Not doctors. (Did anyone's pediatrician ever give successful advice on how to get a full night's sleep?) Not grandparents. (Back in "those days" they simply dipped pacifiers in sugar.) Not the experts who write books. (These experts haven't been parents for many, many years—even *Dr. Spock's Baby and Child Care* still talks about diaper pins!)

Other parents give the best advice. Only parents have the experience—hard-earned experience—that translates into terrific tips, and only parents offer crucial tips such as this:

> *When we arrived the hotel had a crib, but no crib bumpers. So I sent my husband out hunting for bumpers, knowing that the search was probably going to be fruitless—where can you find a crib bumper at 6 P.M. on New York City's Upper East Side? But he came back with padded mailing envelopes, which made perfect bumpers! Our baby slept soundly and safely.*

Unlike any other book, *Outwitting Toddlers* is a compilation of parents' actual experiences. It gives real, down-to-earth information that you can put to use immediately. *Outwitting Toddlers* is also a solution book; it solves the problems that almost every parent encounters. Think of it as being written by not one expert but hundreds. If you want to know the best time to wean your baby from breast to bottle, read Dr. Spock. If you want to know the best way to coax your formerly breast-fed baby into liking formula, read *Outwitting Toddlers*.

The tips in this book were collected by a variety of means. Naturally, we asked our friends, who had more than ample advice to give. On numerous days, employees of Adler & Robin Books, Inc., distributed questionnaires in front of the National Zoo in Washington, D.C., a mecca for parents and their children. Senior researcher Mary Ellen Koenig was relentless in developing and contacting an expanding network of parents who knew other parents around the country. We also posted questionnaires on several national electronic bulletin boards.

Two tips we heard over and over again, so simple when you think about them, are (1) If you have a newborn, sleep every opportunity you can, and (2) Never give your toddler an opportunity to say no.

How we wish we had asked our toddler, Karen, "Do you want your hair or face washed first?" or "Which bedtime story would you like us to read to you?" instead of "Let's wash your hair now" or "Do you want to go to sleep?"

Parents are a funny lot. Humans change through many periods in life: When we learn to walk, we change; when we pass through adolescence, we change; when we go out on our first date, we change; when we complete college, we change. But no change is as dramatic, as powerful, as becoming a parent. All of a sudden we are transformed from party-going, late-night sojourners to boring, sleepy-eyed mothers and fathers who want to spend most conversations talking about diaper-changing strategies. Goodbye *"Saturday Night Live"*; hello *"Sesame Street"*. Our perspective on the entire universe is different the day our son or daughter is born. Better, too.

You'll find some of the tips contradictory. That's okay and normal: Parents can reasonably disagree on the best strategy for dealing with a problem. How to deal with conflicting advice? Of the more than 600 baby and toddler tips contained in this book, just choose the ones that are best for you and your child.

Although not all of the advice may work with your child, at least it's here for the trying.

Baby Equipment

If there's one thing that accompanies any new baby, it's stuff—lots of it. Where do you put it all? In the beginning all your daughter's things might fit nicely in the drawers under her crib. But that quickly changes. Soon you can't walk anywhere in your house without the danger of tripping on a wheeled toy or hearing the sound of Cheerios crunching underfoot. Then there's equipment: strollers, jumpers, walkers, ride-ons, high chairs, booster seats. Read on for ideas on how to keep your child's equipment—and your wits—in place.

Instead of a fixed-size playpen, consider a set of modular units that can be taken apart panel by panel, set up in any number of different shapes including rectangular, circular, triangular, or even run in straight lines or zigzags as a barrier.

Peggy Robin
Washington, D.C.

If your child is into Legos, but you've had it with stepping on those little plastic bricks all over the house, get your child a Lego Bric Vac, a toy that your child slides along the floor. It scoops up the bricks with a paddlewheel motion and collects them in a compartment for storage. You child will enjoy picking up after playtime.

Heather Amsterdam
Brooklyn, New York

We keep a dustpan in our Lego box so that when the kids are finished playing with the zillion little pieces, they just scoop them up.

Eileen Keevan
Hammond, Indiana

Velcro has to be the most useful thing in the parents' universe (after zip-lock bags, of course). I use it everywhere. I put Velcro strips on most of Max's stuffed animals and light plastic toys so that they'll stick to the safety bar of the stroller or to the door of his room or to the back of the car seat or anywhere else I've put a strip of reverse Velcro. I also put Velcro on the undersides of his plates and bowls to stick them to the tray of his high chair. No more fun of picking the plate up and tossing it on the floor for him!

Elaine Danzig
Chicago, Illinois

If you attend any Tupperware parties, there are certain items they offer that are very convenient and can save you money in the long run because they help keep you more organized.

The oval modular containers (size 2) are great for the diaper bag. Use one for cotton balls and tissues and one for powder, lotion, Vaseline, baby Tylenol, a thermometer, Desitin ointment, and so on. Mark the contents on a label on the lid so it's easier to find in the diaper bag.

The plastic lunch boxes are good for Mother's Day Out, day care, or a visit to someone's house. Pack the formula, baby food, cup, and other items inside.

To keep munchies such as Cheerios, use the smallest Tupperware containers with lids.

Sally Tippett Rains
St. Louis, Missouri

I occasionally run a dishwasher full of toys: plastic rattles, teething rings, Fisher-Price people toys, stacking toys—anything that doesn't have paper labels. They come out so clean!

Cathy Shirski
Boston, Massachusetts

Keep a separate changing area near the living room or wherever you spend most of your time. This saves having to run back and forth to the baby's room all the time.

Becky Hagen
Portland, Oregon

We use multicolored Tupperware cups, and each of our four children is assigned her own color. This reduces the number of cups we use every day and also eliminates passing germs around from one child to the other.

Sandy Egan
Princeton, New Jersey

Always keep your diaper bag packed and ready to go. This eliminates part of the getting-out-the-door hassles without having to worry about the diaper bag.

Jean Hutchinson
Takoma Park, Maryland

Luggage stores or variety stores sell a hanging organizer pouch with many zippered compartments, designed to hold jewelry or cosmetics when you travel. But they're so useful for baby things. I hang one on a towel bar right next to the baby's bath so I have easy access to clean cotton balls, Q-tips, baby shampoo, baby washcloths, and other small supplies. I hang another from the headrest behind the front passenger seat in the car, and now I have a place to put little tissue packets, small toys, books, bibs, and other baby essentials for every trip.

Valerie Snow
Baltimore, Maryland

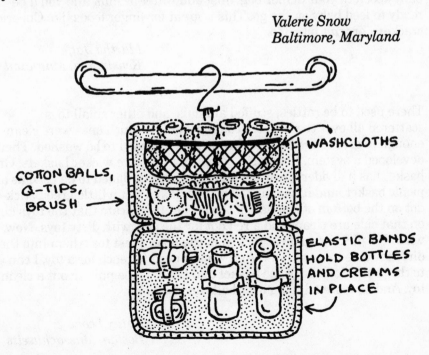

WASHCLOTHS

COTTON BALLS, Q-TIPS, BRUSH →

ELASTIC BANDS HOLD BOTTLES AND CREAMS IN PLACE

I received a lot of cloth diapers before Rachel was born, but I decided to use disposable diapers. I used the cloth ones to put under her chin while feeding her, and the cloth diapers eventually took the place of a security blanket. They were always so soft and smaller than a blanket. Also, since I had a whole pile of them, they were interchangeable and I could easily wash them when they got too dirty from her dragging them around. It worked so well with Rachel that I encouraged Anna and Trisha to use them as security blankets when they were going through that stage.

Lisa Reutzloff
St. Ann, Missouri

Keep the older child's toys in a separate toy bin from baby's things to prevent baby from swallowing smaller parts that are okay for an older child but unsafe for an infant. When the older child is finished playing with her toys, be sure to put everything back in the bin.

Wanda Frank
Boston, Massachusetts

Put dry baby cereal in an empty margarine container and keep it and a baby spoon in your diaper bag. Just add water or milk and you'll be ready to feed baby on the go. This is great for finger foods like Cheerios, crackers, or fruit bits, too.

Martha Jaffe
Kensington, Maryland

There used to be rattles, stuffed animals, and other small toys scattered all over the house. I could never tell which ones were clean enough to give to the baby and which ones needed to be washed. Then I developed a system. I bought a couple of attractive wicker baskets. One basket has a divider down the middle (it was designed to be used as a picnic basket, and it has hinged double lids). I put a little green stick-on dot on the bottom of one half of the basket to indicate that the toys kept on that side are clean, and a red dot for the side with dirty toys. Now, when I'm picking up dirty toys from the floor, I just toss them into the dirty toy side to wash later. And when I need to reach for a toy, I can go to the green-dot side of the basket and know I'll be pulling out a clean toy. And no more tripping over balls and bears!

Kathy Leone
Boston, Massachusetts

Want to start training your children at an early age to pick up their toys? Play "vacuum cleaner baby" with your seven-month or older baby. Hold your baby securely by the waist and lower him head first and hands down toward the floor. At this naturally grabby age a baby almost certainly will reach for and pick up whatever toys he can get his hands on. Once he's gotten hold of a toy, bring him over to the toy box (or wherever you store his toys) and let him drop the toy into the box. Repeat until all the toys are off the floor and put away in their proper places. Pretty soon he'll get the idea that putting his toys away is something he always does at the end of playtime.

Jordan Pollack
Brookline,
Massachusetts

Camping supply stores are full of useful items for babies at home or on the go, and the things you buy there generally cost far less than the same sorts of objects that are specifically designed for babies and sold through infant boutiques and catalogs. Insulated bags make good coolers for traveling with formula or baby food. Small nylon knapsacks make great diaper bags. Fanny packs are good for hands-free carrying of supplies for a short, one-diaper-change trip. Use an ultralight pup tent as a shaded, bugproof backyard playpen. A nylon-covered foam sleeping bag pad can be turned into a bassinet mattress, playmat, or changing pad. Small plastic containers with screw-on lids can carry single-use amounts of diaper-rash lotion, baby food, milk powder, or other necessities. Just walk through the store and use your imagination.

Marilyn Friedman
New York, New York

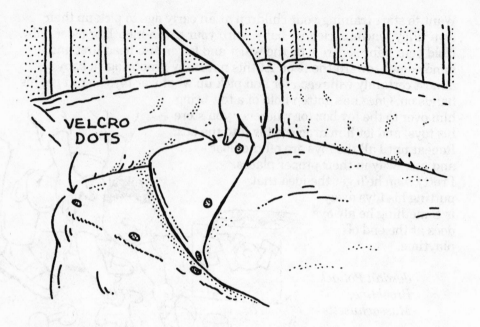

VELCRO DOTS

Changing the fitted sheet on a crib mattress is such a chore! Sam is a big spitter-upper, so on some days I have to change the sheet two or three times. I saw some crib sheets in a baby products catalog that you lay on top of the fitted sheet and attach to the crib bars with Velcro strips, but you still have to remove the crib bumpers to put them on securely. I've come up with a variation that I think works even better. I sewed Velcro dots onto my fitted crib sheet at both ends and along the edges where the bumper rests on the sheet. Then I took a cotton flannel receiving blanket that was about the same length and width as the crib surface and sewed matching Velcro dots on it at the corresponding places. Now when the baby spits up in his crib I just rip off the top sheet and Velcro on a receiving blanket as a new, clean top sheet.

Claire Chin
Walnut Creek, California

If you write to companies and tell them how much you like (or don't like) their products, you often get free products and coupons in return.

Trish Cody
Austin, Texas

Use a backpack instead of a purse. You can fit a lot in it and it can be slung on your back when you need both hands. And husbands are less reluctant to carry a backpack in public.

Various parents

If you live in a small apartment as we do, you'll quickly come to appreciate the need for downsizing baby equipment. Everything seems to be made for people who live in mansions with acres of space. But with a few simple substitutions we've been able to adapt pretty well.

• Use a port-a-crib instead of a full-size crib that you must give away or sell when the baby is too big.

• Instead of a combination carriage/stroller, buy a light umbrella stroller that has a reclining back. Gerry USA makes one that is as light and foldable as most other umbrella strollers but can still recline far enough to be comfortable for a newborn baby.

• In place of a regular high chair, get a booster seat with a feeding tray that you can attach to a regular kitchen chair. If you don't even have room for the feeding tray, you can buy a baby seat that snaps and locks onto your dining table (provided you have the right type of tabletop).

• As a substitute for a separate changing table, use an old, low chest of drawers and turn the top surface into your changing area.

• Instead of a swing on a stand with legs, buy a battery-operated swing seat that sits on the floor or on a tabletop and has a motorized base that gently rocks the swing back and forth. It's called the American Glider Swing and it's made by Evenflo.

Minna Grodin
San Francisco,
California

Bathtime

In the beginning, bathtime may be fun for your baby and for you—or it may not. Some infants love their baths, while others protest vigorously. When we first started giving our daughter, Karen, baths, she sat happily and placidly in the tub—for about a week. From then on, she discovered the joy of making great waves in the tub, imitating a hurricane swell at every opportunity. For Karen, bathtime was a time for one of us parents to wash and the other to dance, sing, make the rubber duck fly through the air—whatever it took to distract her. In this chapter you'll find helpful suggestions from other parents on dealing with the joys of bathtime.

During the bath, float tightly closed bottles of baby lotion in the tub. That way, when you apply the lotion after the bath, it won't feel cold to your baby.

Amy Grant
Dallas, Texas

Our baby is afraid of the bathtub, but she loves mirrors. She'll let us put her in the tub without a fuss if there's a mirror propped up along the side.

Harry Donaldson
Flagstaff, Arizona

Always check the temperature of the bathwater with an elbow or a forearm before placing a child in the tub. It sounds so basic, but in my medical practice, I have seen a number of badly burned babies because the parents did not do that.

Susan Carlson
Alexandria, Virginia

A wet baby is very slippery and can easily be dropped if it's wiggling around. A good trick is to take an old sock and cut holes in it for your fingers to stick through. Hold the baby in that hand and you can get a better grip. Also, keep an apron handy and wear it when bathing the baby.

Maureen Alexander
Chicago, Illinois

I wear sweatbands on my wrist to cover my cuffs; that way I avoid getting my sleeves wet.

Sarah Kaskie
Orlando, Florida

When bathing a baby boy, always lay a washcloth across his penis. He can (and *will*) squirt you—and we're not talking about a little trickle!

Becky Hagen
Portland, Oregon

Whenever our three children started to resist bathtime, we would set the kitchen timer to see who could have the fastest bath and still come out clean.

Sue Poness
Takoma Park, Maryland

I really recommend one of those bath supports for babies who are sitting up. It is made of plastic with a foam-cushion seat and a circular support that surrounds the baby. Suction cups attach to the tub bottom. It keeps the baby secure in the water at all times.

Kitty Berra
St. Louis, Missouri

When my girls resist their baths during the hot, sticky summer, I will occasionally let them have a popsicle in the bathtub. It always gets them in the tub, and it is certainly less of a mess for them to eat the popsicles when they are not wearing clothes!

Patty Bohn
Webster Groves, Missouri

When bathing babies in sinks, always feel the faucet before putting the baby in the water. If hot water was added last, the metal faucet will be very hot and will burn the baby's back, arm, or whatever touches the faucet. Remember to run cold water through the faucet right before putting the baby in.

Eileen Keevan
Hammond, Indiana

We use a "temperature duck" to make sure the baby's bathwater is neither too hot nor too cold. It's a little plastic duck that floats in the water. On its underside is a heat-registering strip that shows the range of temperature that is comfortable and safe for babies. Unlike a glass thermometer, the heat strip is unbreakable, so there's no danger that the baby would get hurt while playing with the temperature duck.

Leslie Verlaine
Bowie, Maryland

I started using the hand-held shower—on the very gentle setting—on my children when they were infants, so they got used to it early and were not afraid of it later. Also, I heard that girls should not sit in dirty water after having their hair washed because it can lead to urinary-tract infections. So I use the hand-held shower first to wash my kids' hair and bathe them—and *then* fill up the bath with clean water so they can play.

Sandra Fletcher
Silver Spring, Maryland

I always had too many baby towels and not enough baby washcloths, so I cut up a few of the towels into small squares.

Diana Cohn
San Francisco,
California

If you don't want to buy a baby support for the bath, use a plastic laundry basket. It serves the same purpose and has other uses.

Renee Schuetter
Kailua, Hawaii

No matter how young, no matter how unadvanced in the language department, no matter how babylike you *think* your baby is, when your little one says "poop" in the bath, *take immediate action.* You've been warned.

And the second time your baby preannounces a poop while in the tub, it's really nobody's fault but yours that you have a mess to clean up.

Bill Adler, Jr.
Washington, D.C.

There's that awkward age when the baby is too big to be bathed in the little plastic baby tub but still too small to sit up in the regular bathtub. My parents told me about a "bathinet," which was a very common piece of baby equipment back when I was small. It's a large basin on a stand that's about waist high. There are usually shelves or drawers underneath. The basin part has a drain hole and hose so you can empty dirty water into a pail or your regular bathtub. You fill the basin with a pail. A pull-down changing pad fits right over the basin, so when the bath is over you can dry and diaper the baby right on top of the bathinet. I don't know why it's so hard to find bathinets nowadays. Apparently, they're very common in Europe. A few baby product stores in New York import them from Italy. Now my baby loves her bath in her own bathinet.

Gloria Goldstein
New York, New York

Our newborn was freaking out when we put her in the bathwater, so we started washing her hair *before* we put her in the water. The gentle head massage makes her pretty mellow and she doesn't thrash around quite so much when she's in the tub.

Jim Mosley
Affton, Missouri

Hair washing is easier and faster if you attach a hand-held shower hose to the tub spout. You can direct the spray and control the pressure of the rinsing stage far better than rinsing with cups of water. You'll get less soap in your baby's eyes, too.

Millie Williams
Bangor, Maine

Those waterproof crib liners that go between the crib sheet and the mattress are also useful at bathtime. I leave one spread out on top of the crib sheet so I'll have a safe place to lay my wet, undiapered baby after the bath. I know I can spend some time gently patting her dry and playing with her and letting her diaper area get some air without worrying that she'll ruin the sheets. Some days when I don't feel like giving her a tub bath, I just take her clothes and diaper off, lay her on the waterproof liner in her crib and give her a quick sponge bath with warm, wet washcloths. I also cut some of the crib liners into quarters to have smaller, more portable waterproof squares to carry in my diaper bag.

Barri Peters
Somerset, Maryland

Bathing my 10-month-old twins has taught me a number of things: (1) Make sure your bathroom floor is well caulked; (2) Wear appropriate clothing, such as a bathing suit or terry-cloth bathrobe; (3) The number of tub toys must be equal to or greater than the number of children to be bathed; and (4) Strawberry- or lemon-scented soaps and shampoos may be mistaken for food.

Janet Orr
Atlanta, Georgia

When our kids were reluctant to have their hair washed, I would give them a hand mirror so they could watch me make wild hairdos with their soaped-up hair. They could also create bubble beards or mustaches on themselves if they liked.

Anne Morrison
Lansing, Michigan

Our toddler hates having his hair washed. It really bothers him to have water in his ears, but he refuses to wear ear plugs. So we let him lie on the kitchen counter with his head over the sink, and we wash his hair in the kitchen sink. The last time we did this, he looked at a book while he lay on the countertop.

Lynn Rawlings
Warson Woods, Missouri

Keep a couple of dry washcloths on hand to dry your baby's face while washing her hair. If you immediately wipe up any water that runs down your child's forehead while wetting, shampooing, or rinsing her hair, then the whole hair-washing procedure will be far less of an ordeal.

Donna Stewart
El Cerrito, California

I use one of those plastic shampoo caps you can order from baby product catalogs or find in some baby stores. It has a rubber visor that sticks out in the front, shielding the eyes from water and soap suds as you rinse.

Linda Barry
Seattle, Washington

I always rinse my baby's hair by sponging the soap off with a damp washcloth instead of pouring water over her head. That's the best way I've found to keep the soap from running down her face and getting in her eyes.

Carol Newcastle
Bethesda, Maryland

Birthdays and Holidays

A first birthday is a wonderful time—well, at least for parents. Even if your child doesn't fully comprehend all the attention being bestowed on him, it doesn't matter. At this very young age, he can be as happy or as angry as he wants without truly ruining the occasion. Unfortunately, this is not so for Thanksgiving and other family holidays. Many a grandparent has invited children and new grandchildren over for an elaborately prepared Thanksgiving feast, only to be told abruptly halfway through the meal, "Sorry, Mom and Dad, Jessie's acting up again; we'd better take him home." Here are some tips for those special occasions throughout the year.

When kids are under five, they have a hard time accepting the idea that only the birthday boy or girl gets the presents. Some parents buy little presents to distribute to all the party guests, but the fact remains that the host's child gets the big haul while the other kids sit and watch—or sit and cry. Here's how to have a happier, more peaceful party. First, when sending out invitations, instruct the parents of the other children that this is a *"no-gift"* party. On the day of the party, give your child his or her presents *before* the little guests arrive. Some parents will no doubt send a gift anyway, but fewer parents will do so if you tell them the reason. Thank the child who brings the gift, then promptly whisk the present out of sight. The party proceeds as usual, with games and small favors for all, and a birthday cake with candles to blow out, but no public display of birthday loot. Save that for when the child is old enough to know how to act pleased even when disappointed by a present, and for when other children are old enough to understand that one day it will be *their* birthday and they'll get the good stuff then.

Marjorie Kastle
Boulder, Colorado

When planning an at-home birthday party, plan twice as many
activities as you think you'll need—they always go faster than you
think they will! Also, don't specify a pick-up time to end the party; tell
the parents that you'll drop the kids off at an approximate time when
the party is finished. This gives you an out when things aren't going
well: "Everyone to the car!"

Anne O'Brien
Sandusky, Ohio

A child's first birthday is really for the parents since the baby could not
care less. So go ahead and have a party, but don't overwhelm the baby
with presents, cameras, and rounds of "Happy Birthday." Let the baby
open one or two presents and quietly sing when it's time for the cake.
It's usually just too much for a baby to handle, and I've seen any
number of babies (including my own) burst into tears on their big day.

Kim Manning
Atlanta, Georgia

Give your child a major hand in preparing for the party. In our
household, the birthday child is always in charge of preparing the treat
bags, which include goodies like stickers, raisins, small games, and a
small amount of candy. The birthday child is also in charge of
distributing the bags when his or her guests leave, and saying "thank
you" to each of them.

Patricia Farrell
Torrance, California

I've found that the best birthday parties are those held away from
home and not dependent on party games. We usually invite a small
number of friends and have cake and ice cream at home first. Then we
go off to do something special: swimming (great at an indoor pool in
January), putt-putt golf, Gymboree, a children's theater production,
and so forth.

Cathy Shirski
Boston, Massachusetts

On each of my children's birthdays, starting the day each was born, I write them a letter. I tell them what they were like that year, what they did, how they acted, and I don't sugar-coat it! I mention their friends, teachers, relatives, as well as any historic events in the family like births, weddings, and deaths. A child's birthday is a perfect milestone to set down your thoughts.

Veronica Campbell
Chesterfield, Missouri

When putting up the Christmas tree with a house full of small children, tie three or four wires or heavy string to the upper trunk of the tree and secure their ends to something stable. We screwed a few small eye-hooks into the wall behind the tree and didn't worry about it falling on top of a small inquiring mind.

Bob Koenig
Takoma Park, Maryland

I make birthday banners out of large pieces of felt hung on colorful plastic hangers. The banners have the child's name, date of birth, and a large felt cake with candles on top. I add small felt candles every year to show how old the child is. You can cut the lettering from felt or simply use the iron-on letters found in most fabric stores. The kids love to hang their birthday banners outside the house on their big day.

Frances Noonan
Kirkwood, Missouri

Make your parties short and sweet. Parties are awfully exciting for preschoolers and too much excitement leads to overstimulation and eventually to crankiness.

Susan Carlson
Alexandria, Virginia

If you have certain rules about what your child can play with, be sure to inform relatives and others likely to buy the child gifts. Tell them well in advance of the birthday. It's too painful for a child to open a box, get a toy gun, and be happy with it, only to have a parent attempt to explain why toy guns aren't allowed.

Kris Dane
Grosse Point, Michigan

Waking up Christmas morning and rushing to open presents can leave a small child overwhelmed. He'll have more fun and be better able to appreciate each new gift if you space them out over the course of the day. Give little stocking stuffers the night before, open the biggest present first thing in the morning, then the presents from Grandma and Grandpa at lunch, and any remaining presents after Christmas dinner. Then the whole day is one of pleasant surprises instead of being all over in the morning present rush.

Gladys McCan
Racine, Wisconsin

Children get so much stuff for their birthdays and special occasions—always too much. We asked the grandparents to send something very small when an occasion warrants a present—and, in addition, to buy our kids a savings bond. By the time our children are college age, they will have a healthy bank balance. And they always have plenty of presents from friends and other relatives for the special events.

Mary Rand
New Orleans, Louisiana

We have accumulated a great collection of holiday books for various occasions: Christmas, Halloween, Easter, Thanksgiving, even Valentine's Day. I keep these books in my closet and only take them out three weeks before the specific holiday. I put them away soon after. It's always a great treat for the kids when the "special books" are brought out every year.

Sarah Kaskie
Orlando, Florida

When Laura was about five, we asked her to design our Christmas cards. She used a pencil to draw a wonderful picture of our family with a Christmas tree. We highlighted the picture with black marker and had it printed on nice paper stock. Before sending them out, Laura and three-year-old Mark colored in the Christmas trees. They were our best Christmas cards ever and we received quite a few comments on them.

Mary Ellen Koenig
Takoma Park, Maryland

To teach very young children to say "thank you" for presents, take a Polaroid picture of the recipient posing with the present and send the photo to the giver. If the child is old enough to write "thank you" or his or her name, include that, too.

Ellen Peters
Springfield, Illinois

When you've got a toddler and a Christmas tree, put the *Christmas tree* in the playpen—everyone and everything is safer that way.

Judy Mosley
Affton, Missouri

It's never too early for a child to learn that Christmas is about giving as well as receiving. For each present that the child opens, he should be taught to give something back. With a two- or three-year old, the only present the child has to give is a hug or a kiss. Older children should make presents for all who give gifts to them. Crayon drawings or finger paintings are good gifts for young children to make. As kids' present-making skills develop, Play-doh bowls or other simple crafts also make fine gifts.

Bill Millin
Racine, Wisconsin

Three- to five-year-olds will love helping you make Christmas cookies. A standard sugar cookie mix is easiest to use.* Let your child smooth out the dough with a rolling pin. Buy cookie cutters in the shapes of ornaments, bells, stars, and trees. Plastic cutters are best so little hands don't get cut. Let your toddler cut the cookies and arrange them in the baking pan himself. He'll feel as if he's a part of the Christmas celebration this way.

Julie Rob
Nashville, Tennessee

---

* Editor's note: Keep children away from raw flour. Uncooked flour can be contaminated with bacteria. You should wash your hands after working with flour.

We needed a way to help our five-year-old cope with conflicting stories about Santa Claus. Some of his friends have been told there is no Santa, while others are 100 percent hooked on all the trappings—flying reindeer, "Ho ho ho," the whole bit. My grandma suggested putting it to him this way: "There is a Santa Claus, but only for children who like to believe in him. As long as you'd like to believe he's there, he will be. One day you may be too old to believe, but that doesn't mean you shouldn't enjoy believing now." Pretty advanced philosophy for a five-year-old, but it did appear to help him with the dilemma.

Dana Garrison
New York, New York

Bottle-feeding

Babies learn about gravity through the bottle more than any other device. It may take your child a couple of tries to realize that the only way to get milk from a bottle is to tilt it upside down. From that moment, it is only natural that a baby soon understands the power of gravity: When you tilt the bottle upside down, without a mouth to catch it, the milk logically pours onto the rug, floor, antique table...Read on for some bottle-feeding tips.

———————

It took me a long while to figure out that life is much easier if you prepare all your bottles first thing in the morning rather than preparing them as needed throughout the day.

Alice O'Neil
New York, New York

This dilemma comes up in the summer months. How do you keep milk fresh in a baby bottle? Unfortunately, you can't. So what I do is carry premeasured powdered milk in a bottle. Then all I have to do is add four ounces of water.

Janice Raisin
San Francisco,
California

Michael spit up a lot, but my pediatrician told me not to change formulas. My mother finally convinced me to try a formula with a lower-iron content, and he was able to tolerate it so much better, which just goes to show that sometimes Mother knows best.

Mary Pat Hennicke
St. Louis, Missouri

Milk spoilage always concerns me. I sometimes pack a bottle of milk when I go out with Alice to the park or the store. I do two things to help make the milk last longer. First, I put it in a cooler designed to hold bottles. Second, I add a drop of Lactaid to the milk. Lactaid is an enzyme that "eats" the lactic sugar in milk. It is this sugar that hastens the spoilage of milk. If you've ever noticed that lactose-reduced milk has a longer shelf life than regular milk, that's why.

Jennifer Dalma
Wilmington, Delaware

How do you wean your baby from a bottle to a cup? First, don't let the baby get in the habit of carrying a bottle around during the day. The bottle becomes a love object, offering emotional comfort, not just a way to drink. Distract the baby with toys or new activities, then quietly remove the bottle.

Katharine Walters
Bethesda, Maryland

Getting your baby to accept liquids cold from the refrigerator will save you a lot of time and hassle. After all, warming bottles is not only time consuming, but it's also a strain when the baby is screaming for milk. Keep using your bottle warmer or a pan of hot water to heat up bottles, but gradually, over the course of two to three weeks, cut down the warming time. Then one day, your baby will love milk cold.

Grace Adams
Bangor, Maine

For convenience and safety I prefer to give Andy his formula cold from the refrigerator, but at first he seemed to prefer it warm. Once he was old enough to hold the bottle himself I discovered he really didn't mind the taste of cold formula—he just didn't like holding a chilly bottle with his fingers. So I bought some small terry-cloth wrist sweatbands and put them around his bottles. They not only keep his little hands from getting cold, but they strengthen his grip on the bottle, too.

Dorothy Harmon
Rockville, Maryland

To switch your one-year-old or older baby from formula to milk: Outfox
your baby's taste buds by starting out with 3/4 formula and 1/4 milk.
When that's accepted, move to 2/3 formula and 1/3 milk, then half and
half. Don't rush the process—eventually you'll have your baby drinking
all milk.

Steve Strang
Lancaster, Pennsylvania

When we were bottle-feeding, a small, portable refrigerator took the
place of my night stand in our bedroom. When it was time for those
late-night feedings, we just reached into the fridge and put the bottle
right into the bottle warmer.

Emily van Loon
Takoma Park, Maryland

Introduce your baby to drinking through a straw instead of trying to
move straight from bottle to cup. You can buy a baby thermos with a
built-in straw that is practically spill-proof. Our daughter just seemed
to get the knack of the straw right away. Now that she's used to getting
her milk or juice from a container other than a bottle, she's less
resistant to the idea of a cup.

Kara Willingham
Brookline, Massachusetts

We decided not to make an issue of Sam's continued use of a bottle,
even though lots of other kids his age were already completely off
bottles and using only cups. Their mothers were always having to
watch out for spills and supervise their drinking. Besides, Sam really
seemed to need the sucking action of the bottle for comfort. He never
used a pacifier and only sucks his thumb to help him go to sleep. I'm
sure that by the time he's three and is a lot steadier with his hands and
can understand better the idea that "bottles are for babies," he will
finally give up the bottle. For now, we spare ourselves the agony of
trying to get him to give up sucking sooner than he'd like.

June C. Young
Seattle, Washington

Introduce the cup fairly early so that when the baby is around 12 months of age, you can get rid of the bottle before it becomes an issue.

Various parents

Juice boxes provide a good transition from bottle to cup. Be sure to buy one of those hard plastic boxes to hold the juice box, so that the baby doesn't squeeze juice all over the place.

Elaine Anderson
Hastings, Nebraska

We never gave our babies warm bottles—they always got them cold right from the refrigerator. It never caused an increase in gas or whatever was supposed to happen.

Also, we would fill some bottles only 3/4 full so that we could freeze them. Whenever we were going to be away from home for a while, we would take a frozen one. By the time the baby wanted a bottle, the milk had thawed out but was still nice and cold.

Sandy Egan
Princeton, New Jersey

Baby bottles come with those tiny plastic caps that you can slide in under the screw-on rings so that you can transport a filled bottle without having to worry about spills. But I've found them to be more trouble than they're worth. When cleaning the bottles, I've dropped that small cap down the garbage disposal more than a few times. Now I just throw them out and use my own method to seal a bottle for travel: Before I screw on the ring and nipple, I stretch a sandwich bag over the top of the bottle. If I use the zip-lock type, I can bring the rest of the bag up over the nipple to make sure it stays clean in my diaper bag.

Emily Ingram
Portland, Oregon

Breast-feeding

What a newborn understands about the breast is that it is the most important source of food, liquid, and comfort. In other words, to a newborn the breast is the most important thing in the world. In this chapter you'll find some helpful hints for breast-feeding your baby.

Lauren had a strong preference for nursing on the left side. To get her to nurse better on the right, I always started feedings on that side, when she was hungriest. First I used a breast pump for a minute or two to pull the nipple out and get the milk flowing. That way she didn't have to work quite so hard on the right as she did to get the milk flow going on the left. Now she's nursing equally from both sides.

Hope Rodbell
Brooklyn, New York

Is there a perfect strategy for weaning a baby from breast to bottle? No, but here's what I did: I offered formula in a cup before each breast feeding. If Sally refused, I offered breast milk expressed in a cup first or tried to mix formula and expressed milk together. This system helped a little, and that was enough!

Terese Taylor
Anaheim, California

If you want to breast-feed, commit yourself to doing it for at least six weeks before deciding whether to stop or not. It usually takes that long for new mothers to work out discomfort or problems that often accompany breast-feeding for the first time. Don't get frustrated—just give yourself enough time.

Kathy Ladd
St. Louis, Missouri

Despite what many breast-feeding experts tell new nursing mothers, it's okay to supplement your nursing with a bottle. I practically starved my first baby because I was "following the rules" so closely. My milk finally came in well enough that my daughter was getting plenty just from me, but don't be afraid to supplement in the beginning.

Nancy Tanner
McLean, Virginia

Chew gum when you are first breast-feeding—it helps get your mind off the initial discomfort and gives you something to clamp down on when you experience more than discomfort.

Judy Mosley
Affton, Missouri

Babies, especially newborns, need to nurse many times during the day. Often, this is the only time that mothers get to sit down, put their feet up, and relax. Make sure you have a drink of your choice handy when you start feeding. Your baby will be content if you remember to make eye contact with him or her.

Martha Shirk
Webster Groves, Missouri

Instead of buying disposable nursing pads to catch drips when I was breast-feeding, I simply used my husband's clean white handkerchiefs. They were equally absorbent and could be used over and over again.

Veronica Campbell
Chesterfield, Missouri

To encourage the start of your milk-flow (the "letdown reflex") while expressing milk, tape your baby "talking" or listen to music that reminds you of your baby. I would listen to Windham Hill and Bach tapes when expressing milk at work—it really helped ease the emotional letdown. Also, I would bring photos of the baby to help.

Susan Robinson
St. Louis, Missouri

For sore nipples, I sometimes applied a warm compress of used tea bags, followed by a thorough airing. It seemed to help.

Maureen Alexander
Chicago, Illinois

This is so basic, but it took me a while to figure out: When you're nursing, do not wear blouses that button down. Instead, wear loose tops that can be pulled up. You are much less exposed that way.

Trish Cody
Austin, Texas

My newborn daughter was a small eater, so in the beginning I was nursing her every two and a half hours around the clock! I was exhausted until I started taking her to bed with me and putting a rolled-up beach towel behind her to prop her up and keep her safe. I would catnap as she fed, switch sides, and then return her to her crib when she was done feeding. We were both much happier with this solution.

Gresham Lowe
Takoma Park, Maryland

When you are first breast-feeding and you have enough milk in one breast to satisfy your baby, have a cup or something ready to catch the milk that drips (or in my case, spurts) from the other breast. This way you can store your own milk without much effort.

Arlene Gottlieb
Silver Spring, Maryland

Positioning the baby correctly can really help when you have sore nipples. Don't hold the baby so that she is pulling down on your breast. Rather, hold her up higher and position her so that she is facing directly into the breast—there's much less pull.

Cathy Shirski
Boston, Massachusetts

When it's time to switch a baby from one breast to the other, be sure you break the child's suction by inserting your finger into the side of his or her mouth. Otherwise, trying to pull the baby off your breast will lead to sore nipples.

Pat Slater
Takoma Park, Maryland

To keep track of which breast you, or rather the baby, used last, keep a plastic paper clip on your bra strap. Put the clip on the side you're currently using.

Various mothers

I bought a few nursing bras, but they were terribly expensive. They got stained at the tip of the cups from milk leakage, were hot and didn't allow air to flow to my sore nipples, and never fit as well as my regular bras. Who needs that? So I went back to wearing good, regular support bras, but I cut holes around the nipples and sewed up the edges to keep the fabric from unraveling. Now I don't have to fumble with the openings when I'm ready to nurse the baby.

Tina Hunter
Silver Spring, Maryland

Here's one way to help wean the baby off the breast: offer fruit juice in a cup. Once the cup is accepted as a way to drink, then try substituting whole milk. If the baby is under 12 months, offer formula.

Janice Workman
Washington, D.C.

If you intend to go back to work but want to continue breast-feeding, get your baby accustomed to sucking from an artificial nipple when he's still under three months old and able to accept new feeding techniques. At least once a day, offer expressed milk in a bottle. (This will also help you learn to express more efficiently so that by the time you do start work, you'll be good at it.) However, to avoid nipple confusion and to make sure that the breast-feeding routine is well established, you should wait until the baby is at least three weeks old before offering a bottle.

Joyce Nielson
New York, New York

You can special order clothes with specially designed, well-hidden nursing openings, but I've found it's easiest to wear loose cotton sweaters and roomy tent-tops. Drape a big print scarf or shawl over your shoulders for a slightly dressier look—it's also great for covering you up so that you can nurse discreetly in restaurants or other public places.

Virginia Tievsky
Beltsville, Maryland

On weaning: Eliminate breast-feedings gradually, cutting down no more than one a week, starting with the midday feeding and then cutting out the one in the afternoon and then the midmorning feeding. Eliminate the last breast-feeding in the evening and the first breast-feeding in the morning in the final two weeks of the program.

Lucy Lana
Cincinnati, Ohio

First-time nursing mothers are almost always bothered by sore nipples in the beginning. La Leche League is a network of local support groups run by volunteers who hold regular meetings at which mothers come together and discuss aspects of breast-feeding and infant care. The following sore-nipple remedies came out of a recent La Leche League meeting: applying Vitamin E oil or pure anhydrous lanolin cream; rubbing breast milk around the nipple after each nursing; using a blow dryer on a low or moderate setting rather than towel drying the breasts; exposing the nipples to sunlight; using warm or cool compresses; and varying nursing positions at each feeding so that the baby doesn't exert constant pressure on the same part of the nipple each time.

Various mothers

Car Trips and Car Seats

Babies were meant to ride in cars. Practically every parent learns that sometimes the only way to get a three-week-old to sleep is to put the baby in the car and take a midnight drive around the block a couple dozen times. But when you're taking your baby on longer trips, you'll certainly need more than just the infant or toddler car seat: diapers, formula, tissues, wipes, towels, toys, shades for the windows. And once you're done packing for overnight trips, you may discover that you're hauling the baby's entire nursery into your car. We know one family that has to take their son's mattress on car trips because he will sleep only on that mattress. Other stories and suggestions are included in this chapter.

———————

When taking a long car trip, I wrap small items—boxes of raisins, coloring books, note pads, stickers, and so forth—and then set designated times to open them: every two hours, every hour, whatever. It gives my kids something to look forward to.

Sally Tippett Rains
St. Louis, Missouri

Everyone *must* go to the bathroom before getting in the car. This is not simply for my convenience as a parent, it's for our children's safety as well. My daughter was in a serious car accident when she was four and, although she was wearing a seat belt, she sustained severe internal injuries, mostly because her bladder was full at the time of the accident. Now, *everyone*—including adults—must "go" before the car goes.

Patty Noonan
Kirkwood, Missouri

Singing in the car is a great way to pass the time and settle down a fussy child. Go for the songs that involve everyone, such as "Old MacDonald Had a Farm" or "If You're Happy and You Know It." As the kids get older, you can do rounds like "Row, Row, Row Your Boat" or longer songs like "Ninety-nine Bottles of Beer on the Wall."

Various parents

The best investment we made for car trips was a cassette player with a headset for *each* of our daughters. That way they can each listen to the music and stories they want to hear—and my husband and I can talk.

Laurie Potts-Dupre
College Park, Maryland

We use an old diaper-wipe box to collect removable plastic stick-ons from various sources: discarded Colorform sets, fast-food restaurant giveaways, and others. When we take long car trips we bring along the box, and the kids plaster the stick-ons on the windows, making up new stories or just decorating the car.

Patricia Farrell
Torrance, California

We use old lunchboxes to store small toys for car rides. We always take Matchbox cars, crayons, anything small. And we always have extra lunchboxes because either the thermos breaks or the kids simply want new boxes every year.

Mary Anne Hess
Silver Spring, Maryland

For long trips, we usually leave at 4 or 5 A.M. and put the kids directly in the car in their p.j.'s with their pillows and blankets. They will sleep at least two or three hours. Then we pull out a "10 o'clock grab bag"— the kids get to pick from a shopping bag of little wrapped presents at 10 A.M. and every two hours afterward—for good behavior.

Suzanne Fleming
Takoma Park, Maryland

Always carry a small pillow for *each* child in the car—not just for car trips but at all times. When they are infants, the pillow can be used to prop their heads up. When they are older, they can lay their heads on them. Your kids can use pillows to "mark territory" between them or use them as soft desks. Decorative pillows are relatively inexpensive at places like Pier 1 Imports or discount linen stores (although many of these inexpensive pillows get lumpy after washing).

Ellen Peters
Springfield, Illinois

Where we live there's a lending program for infant car seats. The local government's general information line had the number for the program. I called about a month before my wife had the baby and, for a 10-dollar refundable deposit, was able to borrow a perfectly good infant car seat for a year. By the time Kevin was a year old, he was over 20 pounds and so was ready for a forward-facing toddler seat. We didn't have to buy two different seats or try to prop him up or arrange padding so that he could fit comfortably in one of those convertible infant/toddler seats. I know there are a lot of towns, counties, and states that have similar lending programs. Some of the big car insurance companies lend car seats, too.

Peter Weiss
Washington, D.C.

On long car trips, we would always look for a playground after dinner and allow the kids to let off steam for an hour or so. Then we would get them into their p.j.'s and drive until midnight. When we got to the hotel, we could take them straight to bed.

Dee Raff
Takoma Park, Maryland

We pack the kids' clothes in pillow cases for car trips. Each child has a different-colored pillow case so we can tell them apart. The cases are secured with rubber bands and used as pillows during the car trips.

Frances Noonan
Kirkwood, Missouri

Always keep an extra set of clothes, including underwear and socks, in your car for each of your children.

Nancy Tanner
McLean, Virginia

Cosco makes a safe car bed/seat for infants under 17 pounds. It's very useful if you have a baby like ours who, until five months, hated being propped up in seats or strollers and was only happy lying down.

Julie Wilson
Albany, New York

If you want to protect your car's upholstery from marks caused by the car seat frame or from your baby's drools and dribbles (or worse), look for an auto splat mat. It's a plastic mat that covers the back seat but has cut-outs for the seat belts. We found this item in the *One Step Ahead* baby products catalog, but you can also make one yourself very easily. Just buy a full-size waterproof crib pad, spread it over the back seat, mark the points at which the seat belts would come through, and cut slits in the pad so that you can fasten the car seat securely. It won't look quite as nice as the ready-made splat mat, but it will do the job just as well.

Lee Culver
Tarrytown, New York

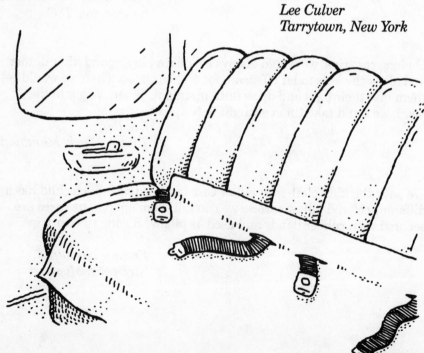

Always keep a spare diaper in the glove compartment of the car.

Patty Noonan
Kirkwood, Missouri

When the car is parked in the sun during the summer, the car seat buckle gets so hot I'm afraid to put the baby in and risk having her skin get burned from contact with the metal. But now I keep a small jug of water and a washcloth in the car. Before I put the baby in, I wipe down the car seat buckle with the wet washcloth and that cools it off well enough to put her in without danger. I also carry a couple of Wash 'n Dries in my purse: they do the same job.

Debby Allen
Queens, New York

I keep a receiving blanket in the car to cover the car seat and keep it cool when the car is parked in an unshaded spot.

Michael Richards
Boston, Massachusetts

Before you go out and spend a lot of money on a car seat, it's worth taking the time to think about how it will fit your individual travel needs. Since all car seats must meet federal standards, they're all safe if used according to directions. Ask yourself:
• How easy is it to adjust the straps each time the baby is put in?
• As the baby grows, how easy is it to readjust the straps to the next level up?
• How well will the car seat fit in the back seat of the model car that you have? (Some compacts have back seats that are too small for the larger type of car seat.)
• Do you have a two-door car? If so, you may want the Renolux Turn-a-tot, which swivels to one side, allowing you to lift the baby out without a lot of bending and twisting.
• Will you use the car seat for air travel? You may want one that has a carrying handle, is fairly lightweight, or can be strapped onto your luggage cart in a stable manner.

Karen Harris
Takoma Park, Maryland

When your baby is still in a rear-facing infant seat, he doesn't have a very good view. Our baby was often cranky and bored, staring at the back seat of the car on every trip, until I made a back-seat storyboard for him. I went to a toy store and bought a set of Colorforms. They'll stick to a sheet of plastic or vinyl that you can buy in any good art supply or hardware store. I attached the vinyl sheet to the back seat so that my baby looks right at it when his car seat is in place. When my husband is driving and I'm sitting in the back seat next to the baby I can arrange scenes and make up stories to keep him amused as we're

traveling. I can rearrange the Colorforms endlessly to make new pictures, so he doesn't get bored. It's so much safer than letting him play with loose toys that could easily cause an injury in a car accident. By the time he's old enough to reach out and try to pull off the Colorforms, he'll be old enough for a forward-facing seat and can enjoy the view out the car window.

Vicki Panayotis
Newport News, Virginia

We have friends who bought three different car seat models before they found one that was both easy to operate and comfortable for their baby. To avoid that problem I took our baby to the store (in our friends' borrowed car seat, of course) and put him into each of the car seat models that were on display. I tried to put him in from the side just as I would have to do if the seat was in a car. My baby found one so comfortable that he fell asleep in it at the store. That's the car seat I bought.

Lucy Washington
Bethesda, Maryland

In taking long car trips with a baby who sleeps through the night, the best time to leave is just at the baby's bedtime. With luck, your baby will fall asleep as the trip begins and stay that way until you arrive at your destination or have to take a comfort break.

Lucy Lighton
Bethesda, Maryland

After messing around with expensive car seat shades, car window shades that can't be adjusted to deal with the shifting sun, and those thick vinyl stick-on shades that are hard to see through, I finally found the perfect solution: tinted plastic food wrap! You can get it in rolls of blue or green. I keep a roll in the car, zip off a sheet, and stick it to the back-seat window on the right or left, depending on the position of the sun. A few extra layers are necessary when the sun is especially glaring. Just peel the plastic wrap off and throw it out when you don't need it anymore.

Dean Ready
Boston, Massachusetts

Clothing

arly on, parents make several discoveries about baby clothing. The size that is marked on the clothes has no connection with the real world of baby sizes. There are two kinds of clothes—the kind that is easy to remove for a diaper change, and the kind that is not. It's silly to buy any baby clothing that must be handwashed. Finally, your baby really does feel ridiculous in that bunny suit with the big ears. Read on for other discoveries.

I used to go crazy buying baby clothes. None of the sizes matched my baby's size: Most of the 24-month-old clothing didn't even fit my 13-month-old. It must be some kind of conspiracy. But here's how I solved this problem. I put my baby down on a large sketching pad and drew an outline of his body in crayon. Then I cut out the outline, folded it up neatly, and put it in my pocketbook. Whenever I'm out buying clothes without the baby, I just hold up the outline to the clothes and get a pretty good idea of how well they'll fit. I also made copies of the outline and gave them to both sets of grandparents. (You'll have to draw new outlines periodically as your child grows.)

Joanna Berman
Charlottesville, Virginia

Have a child-size coat rack for the children's coats. It really makes my girls feel like big kids when they can hang up their own coats, and it's a help to me.

Kathleen Winters
Tempe, Arizona

It took me two years to find out about it, but Shout takes out almost any kind of stain.

Laurie Palmer
Takoma Park, Maryland

Have a separate chest of drawers for larger-size clothes, whether they be hand-me-downs or presents that are too big. When my older son, Mark, grows out of clothes, they go directly into a chest of drawers in Christopher's closet, with the sizes marked on the outside of each drawer.

Eileen Keevan
Hammond, Indiana

When you get baby clothes—whether new or hand-me-downs—hang them up in the closet in graduating lengths, not by sizes. You will be less likely to pass over some of the clothes because the baby grows past the particular size or because the sizes aren't accurate.

Elaine Anderson
Hastings, Nebraska

I couldn't bear to give away all my baby booties and mittens when the babies outgrew them (and in some cases, there was only one left anyway), so I sewed a loop on some of them and hang them on the Christmas tree every year.

Anne Morrison
Lansing, Michigan

To teach a toddler how to put on her own coat, have the child lay the coat face-up at her feet so that the collar touches her shoes. The child bends over, puts her hands into the arm holes, and then swings the coat up over her head. It's on—not backward, not upside down, but on right!

Jim Noonan
Kirkwood, Missouri

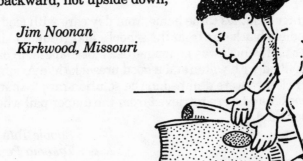

When we are going anywhere, whether on a trip or just to Grandma's house, I gather a complete change of clothes for each child and put them together with a large safety pin. This saves me—or whoever is caring for my kids—from rummaging through diaper bags or suitcases looking for underwear and socks.

> *Barb Schiller*
> *St. Louis, Missouri*

Here's a recipe for getting formula stains out of baby clothes, even after they've been in storage for two or three years: Mix together in a sink or plastic bucket (don't use aluminum) a gallon of hot water, 1/4 to 1 cup of dishwasher detergent (like Cascade), and 1/4 cup bleach (check labels on clothing as to whether bleach is safe to use). Dissolve ingredients and soak clothes for 30 minutes. Then wash normally in the washing machine.

> *Kim Manning*
> *Atlanta, Georgia*

We used to endure many temper tantrums about clothing with our toddlers until I developed the habit of laying out three choices every morning and letting the child pick what he or she wanted to wear. This seemed to allow enough autonomy so that the "problem" was no longer a big deal.

> *Gresham Lowe*
> *Takoma Park, Maryland*

My daughter's clothes came home from day care with food stains and this incredible black dirt from the school's playground. I simply kept my diaper pail (which was no longer used for diapers) in our upstairs bathroom filled with water and a good presoak (like Axion). Every night, her clothes were dumped in the solution rather than a dirty clothes basket and were retrieved from the diaper pail when it was time to do laundry.

> *Bobbie Tate*
> *Takoma Park, Maryland*

No matter how careful you are with bibs, your toddler is going to get food stains on her clothes. Carrots, beets, and sweet potatoes are the hardest spots to remove once they've set. I got tired of changing Jennifer's clothes after every meal with these foods. Now I look for clothes that have orange or red flowers on them, or have crazy-quilt splotches of red or yellow as part of the fabric design. When she's wearing these clothes, I don't worry about food stains because they blend right in with the pattern.

Carol Rice
New Castle, Delaware

Resale shops, consignment shops, and special sales of just-kids-clothing are the best places to buy clothes, particularly big-ticket items such as coats and dress-up clothes.

Various parents

Buy the one-piece p.j.'s without feet for infants; you get more wear out of them.

Patty Noonan
Kirkwood, Missouri

I want Julie to wear a scarf and mittens on a cold day, but she's at that stage where she just says no to whatever I suggest. However, I don't give her the opportunity to reject the warm clothes; instead, I give her an array of choices. I pull out three scarves and two pairs of mittens. Then it's up to her to pick which ones she'll wear. She loves being able to make her own choices, and I love not having to fight with her every time she wants to go out in the cold.

Caryn McFarlane
Van Nuys, California

I use Vivid, a denture cleaner, to get formula stains out of baby clothes. Just dissolve the mixture and soak the clothes before washing.

Nancy Tanner
McLean, Virginia

During the summer, most babies really need only a diaper and a T-shirt. You can dress up a plain white T-shirt by stenciling a cute design on it using fabric paints.

Mary Pat Hennicke
St. Louis, Missouri

I keep clothes that are not being used (because they are either too big or too small) in clear, zippered bags—the kind comforters and blankets come in. I mark the sizes on the outside of the bag.

Sandra Fletcher
Silver Spring, Maryland

When Shannon was about three years old, we were having trouble getting her to change her underwear often enough. We finally figured out that she would wear only her two pink pairs. So I dyed all of her underwear pink, and that solved the problem.

Sandy Egan
Princeton, New Jersey

Bathing suits for babies still in diapers are more trouble than they're worth. And they're so expensive! I stopped struggling to put a bathing suit on over a bulky diaper and now just put my toddler in a cloth diaper (the paper ones tend to disintegrate after full immersion) and put a pair of plastic pants over the diaper for protection. For extra protection against sunburn I often put a T-shirt on the baby before I put her in the pool.

Sarah Morris
Concord, California

Everyone has extra mufflers and warm scarves. If you're visiting friends or relatives and the weather suddenly turns cold, don't ask to borrow a bulky adult blanket. Just wrap the baby in a borrowed knit scarf—it's so much easier to return, too.

Jennifer Coleman
Old Saybrook,
Connecticut

When the baby was growing so quickly, I didn't bother buying him a snowsuit. Instead, I bought some of those extra-furry sleepers in several sizes. They are less expensive than snowsuits, plenty warm, and I got several to fit him during those months of quick growth.

Grace Schiller
St. Louis, Missouri

Don't bother buying winter p.j.'s for your kids—just let them wear old warm-ups.

Diana Cohn
San Francisco,
California

You can buy crotch extenders, which will almost double the wearing time of your baby clothes. It's a piece of cotton fabric with a set of snaps on each side that will give about two more inches of length when you snap them onto the baby's rompers or playsuits. If you can't find them in a baby products store or variety store, look for them in major baby mail-order catalogs, or you can even make them yourself.

Lena Stein
Oakland, California

Getting shoes on your toddler is a learned skill. With one hand, loosen the shoe and hold the tongue up all the way. With the other hand, grasp your child's heel firmly and point her toes in toward the front of the shoe, pushing down on her heel until the heel is in. Don't bother buying laced shoes; get Velcro, so you'll have a shot at closing the shoes before your child wanders off.

Doris Land
Elizabeth, New Jersey

I never let the salesman put shoes on our toddler. She thinks all strangers who want to handle her body are doctors. I always put the shoes on her myself; this makes for a happier time at the shoe store.

Peggy Robin
Washington, D.C.

Some toddlers like shopping for shoes, others don't—and they let you know it! If your child cries when having her foot sized, ask the store clerk if you can measure your baby's feet. If the clerk says, "No, the measurement must be made by a professional," or something like that, you have two choices. Either go to another store, or estimate your child's shoe size and simply try on that size. As for width, no one brand fits like another, so measuring width on a small child's feet doesn't help much anyway.

Bill Adler, Jr.
Washington, D.C.

When first learning to crawl or walk, your baby will be hampered by booties that fall off or are too slippery. Don't rush your child into real shoes too soon. Instead:
• Let your child wear only snug-fitting socks with rubber no-skid treads on the bottom.
• Put your child in one-piece rompers that have feet attached and let him walk on carpeted or other nonslick surfaces.
• Buy a pair of soft, leather baby moccasins that have laces and come up over the ankle. (These can be kicked off, but it takes a lot of determination.)
• Buy snap booties that fit snugly.
• Leave your child barefoot whenever weather and surface permit.

Denise Williamson
Dallas, Texas

I buy all my kids' clothes way too big. Sooner or later they grow into everything. And cotton clothes will always shrink smaller than you expect. In the meantime, it's so easy to roll up the sleeves and cuffs.

Martha Howell
Olney, Maryland

I couldn't find any mittens small enough to stay put on the hands of my two-month-old, but I found that her smallest, tightest pair of socks worked very well.

Nancy Pratt
Bakersfield, California

Bundling a small baby in coats and snowsuits is always a chore and usually results in a bout of crying. I just take the baby, normally dressed, and put him in my Snugli front carrier. Then I put on my biggest and bulkiest coat and button it up around the baby, leaving the top buttons undone to let air circulate. That way we're both warm and toasty on our winter walk.

Sally Newman
Burke, Virginia

Colic

ow do they do it? How do children scream for hours and hours without stopping, without getting hoarse, without seeming to breathe in between? And why? Do they want to get back in the womb? Watch the late movie? Nobody knows for certain what causes colic and nobody knows how to cure it. But as you'll see in this chapter, there are remedies that last for as long as half an hour, and half an hour of quiet can seem like a gift from the gods.

Lay your very young baby tummy-side down over your forearm, head resting in the palm of your hand, arms and legs dangling free. Our doctor told us this was called "the colic hold."

Mark Bausch
Middletown, Connecticut

Hal had an extreme form of colic, something medically known as *hypertonic*. It went on for longer than typical colic. Eventually, we learned to make his environment "soft" and that seemed to help: low lights, quiet surroundings, and minimal clothes. We also learned to avoid going up and down stairs with him because, for some reason, the movement of stepping up or down caused him to throw back his arms and head in the startle reflex—it just seemed to set him off.

Terry Clifford
Takoma Park, Maryland

Turn all the lights out at once and plunge the baby into sudden, complete darkness. All crying will stop—at least for a moment.

David Mallory
Washington, D.C.

For an infant with colic, lay a lambskin pad on top of your clothes dryer, lay the baby on the pad on her stomach, and turn on the dryer, keeping a firm hand on the baby's back. Pull up a chair and get comfortable, if you like.

Gloria Schwarz
Des Peres, Missouri

Warm a receiving blanket in the dryer for a short time and wrap it around the baby's tummy. This seems to help comfort the baby, and lets the parent feel like he or she is doing something to help.

Sue Klein
Takoma Park, Maryland

We laid Lauren in a buggy and rolled her over the uneven surface where the carpet ended and the hardwood floor began. The back-and-forth movement, along with the consistent bumping, helped her quiet down.

Sue Poness
Takoma Park, Maryland

We taped sounds from our home environment (dishwasher, vacuum cleaner, clothes dryer, and so forth). Playing them back quieted the baby. The monotony seems to comfort a colicky baby.

David Band
Takoma Park, Maryland

We give the baby "gripe juice" (available from health food stores); this is a concoction that, when given to babies in small doses, helps relieve gas pains.

Sue Klein
Takoma Park, Maryland

Try a baby massage. Chris loves to get one and is quiet as long as the massage is going on.

> *Di Hellman*
> *New York, New York*

While nursing or feeding the baby, place a heating pad—set on medium—on the baby's mattress. Remove the pad before putting the baby down. A warm place for the baby's tummy always seems to do the trick.

> *Ellen Kruger Erbe*
> *Kirkwood, Missouri*

We'd sit our baby in her seat, face her toward the television, and turn on MTV at a moderately high volume (too loud will hurt the baby's ears). The heavy-metal videos especially seemed to lull her into a trancelike state.

> *Lou Binder*
> *Brooklyn, New York*

Try a Snugglehead, a pillow that cradles the area around the top of your baby's head. The baby's head doesn't rest on it, so there's no danger of suffocation. It gives the baby the secure feeling of being back in the womb and helps the baby go to sleep.

> *Patricia Robinson*
> *Berkeley, California*

Keep your baby upright for at least half an hour after feeding. This way, gas pains, often a cause of colic, are less likely to appear.

> *David Jefferson*
> *Bridgton, Maine*

Play music, loud enough at first for the baby to hear over his own wails.

> *Susan O'Dell*
> *Ames, Iowa*

Hold the baby up to a fish tank, if you have one. It's a simple, soothing change of scenery.

Harlan Cadell
Rockville, Maryland

Step outside for a moment with the baby. A bit of bracingly cold air, especially in winter, will calm the baby down.

Martha Jaffe
Kensington, Maryland

Put your baby in a bassinet with unbreakable mirrors on all sides. The baby will be fascinated to see other babies everywhere and may even coo and smile.

Alice Hampton
Scarsdale, New York

I use the baby's stroller as the main colic-calming device. I have one with a back that can go down flat to become a carriage, and in the evenings when the baby is at her fussiest, I put her in it and wheel her around the house or around the yard, pushing as fast as I can. When we have dinner I wheel the stroller into the dining room and eat with one foot resting on the rear axle, rocking it back and forth. The stroller usually gives us at least 10 minutes of quiet a night, and if we're lucky, our baby falls asleep in it, and we leave her resting there until she wakes up to be fed several hours later.

Jill Schott
Cincinnati, Ohio

Sarah loves a warm bath, so whenever she's especially colicky, we prepare her tub and hold her in it for as long as she likes, even if that means my hands turn into prunes.

Courtney Rischer
White Plains, New York

Get a loud-ticking kitchen timer or old-fashioned clock and put it near the baby's crib or bassinet. The constant sound calms the baby down. I discovered this by accident, but it really works.

Lisa Morton
New York, New York

Turn the TV on to an unused channel. The sound of the static combined with the snowy, grainy picture has a hypnotic effect.

Tedd Anderson
Chicago, Illinois

Rolling credits at the end of a TV movie have a calming effect on Nicholas. He also gazes in fascination at the financial ticker that runs along the bottom of the TV screen during the business report segment on CNN.

Patty Schleffer
Berkeley, California

When Sarah is crying for no discernible reason, I open my mouth wide and cry "Waaaaaaaaah" right back at her. Sometimes that surprises her into silence for a few moments.

Julie Schultz
Great Neck, New York

My doctor said Elise would be less colicky if I stopped nursing her on demand and made her wait three hours between the beginning of one feeding and the start of the next. I was skeptical at first and found it hard to listen to her cry when I knew she wanted milk, but once she got used to the schedule, evenings with her really did go much better.

Sherry Goodman
Chicago, Illinois

Vigorous rocking worked best with Kristen. We bought a battery-powered baby swing, so we wouldn't always be jumping up to crank the swing. Then we saw a wind-up model that really had a powerful, long-lasting rocking motion, so we bought a second swing. Then we learned that Evenflo makes a portable swing that we can take with us to Grandma's house and use on vacation. Those three swings have made our lives a lot quieter.

Dan Vondel
Arlington, Virginia

Car rides worked for our baby, and we actually did take him out for some midnight drives, but of course he was awake and crying as soon as we came home. We sent for a car-ride simulator that makes the crib vibrate and hum like a moving car, and that helped... some of the time.

Wendy Blake
Los Angeles, California

In David's case, the cause was clearly gas. He seemed to be in pain after nursing because he couldn't burp easily. So I just kept patting and rubbing him in different positions for 10, 20 minutes at a time, as long as it took to bring up the air bubble that was bothering him.

Elizabeth Hazzmi
Cleveland, Ohio

Although it may last only minutes, one temporary cure for colic is to put the baby over your shoulder and dance around the room, singing.

Carl Daye
Winchester, Virginia

Day Care and Preschool

Day care and preschool are signs of advanced toddlerhood. Some toddlers accept these events with grace and joy; others protest as vigorously as they know how. As we'll see in the following responses, day care and preschool are often more trying on parents than they are on kids.

Visit the day-care center more than once, *unannounced,* to check things out before you enroll your child. If the center doesn't allow parents to pop in and see what's going on without an appointment, go to another center.

Pay special attention to the diaper-changing procedures that you see. Poor staff hygiene practices, such as not washing hands after changing a baby, are a major cause of infection among day-care attendees. The changing table *must* be cleaned with bleach after each child's change, or a fresh paper cover must be put down.

Be sure that the center has clear rules about sick children. Unless parents are forbidden from bringing in toddlers who have a case of the sniffles or the flu, you can be sure that your child will be coming home with a cold every other week.

Find out how staffers are hired. Is there a background check? Are personal references necessary? Are CPR and first-aid training required? Does everyone speak English well enough to be understood by a 9-1-1 operator? If you don't get a yes to all of these questions, keep looking!

Various parents

To reduce the hassle of everyone getting out the door on time in the morning, we have a firm rule: No breakfast until you are fully dressed.

Patty Bohn
Webster Groves, Missouri

Let your child bring a favorite toy, stuffed animal, or blanket to the day-care center.

Leslie Wells
Seattle, Washington

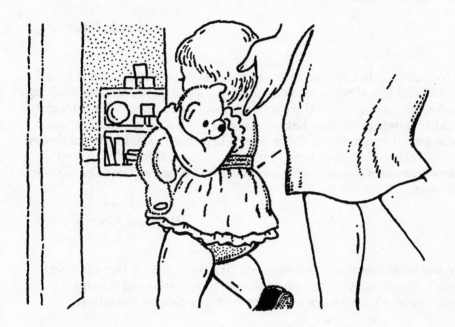

Toddlers often cry the first few times they're dropped off at preschool because they are afraid to be left in unfamiliar surroundings. Try this as a preventive measure: Get to know parents of toddlers the same age who are about to attend or already attend the chosen preschool. Let the children play together and become used to seeing one another. The first day of preschool, drop them off together and none of them will feel so alone, since they have a little friend or friends close by.

Margaret Samuels
Albany, New York

To prevent first-day separation terror, stay most of that first day with your child. That way you can also satisfy yourself that the center is well run and appropriate for your child's level of development.

Various parents

Choose a center that has a really great playset—a big, fun slide, good baby swings, a whirlaround, and other equipment that you don't have at home. Then your child will want to go to the center because that's where the fun stuff is. Don't buy better equipment yourself or you'll ruin the center's main source of attraction.

> *Alice Grant*
> *Evanston, Indiana*

If your child is in day care or preschool, you've probably already heard about head lice, if not already dealt with them and the endless washing that accompanies them. During the school year, I always blow-dry my children's hair after their baths because I have a theory that if they have picked up anything, the heat will help destroy it. It's only a theory, but after three kids and nine years of preschool, kindergarten, and elementary school, our family has never had a case of head lice. Knock on wood.

> *Becky Hagen*
> *Portland, Oregon*

On weekend mornings, I always say: "It's Saturday (or Sunday). No school! No office!" Our daughter likes to repeat that and it helps her understand where we are when she is at day care on weekdays.

> *Nancy Nathan*
> *Bethesda, Maryland*

I always keep a snack of juice, crackers, and fruit in the car for my daughter when I pick her up from day care. It always makes life easier, particularly when I have to run errands after work. It really came in handy one time when we were stuck in traffic for hours because of a freak snowstorm.

I also keep supplies at my office for those unexpected emergencies when day care or school is closed for some reason (usually weather-related). I keep an exercise mat, pillow, and blanket for my daughter to take a nap on, and I always keep an "entertainment kit" on hand and well supplied with scissors, tape, paper, a chalk board, and so on.

> *Bobbie Tate*
> *Takoma Park, Maryland*

A major problem for all parents is what to do with the steady stream of artwork constantly flowing into the house from day care or preschool. There's no way you can display it all, and there's no way you can save it all. I finally got a box for each of my kids' closets, and now *they* save what they want. We look at all the pictures together after school and then they decide what they want to keep and what they want to throw away. I'm off the hook for those tough decisions, and they keep the piles of work in their closets and out of the way.

Debbie Marklin
Reading, Pennsylvania

Diaper Time

Anytime changing a diaper seems like a chore, remember this: There are parents who are dealing with twins, triplets, and even more. Changing diapers may not be fun, but the alternative is even less pleasant. The key to surviving diaper time is not enduring the odor, it's keeping the baby in one place and keeping him from using his stuffed animal or blanket to explore what's going on down there. Here are some helpful tips from the diaper-changing experts themselves—parents.

Ever have a fussy toddler on the diaper-changing table? Put a pack of flash cards or playing cards with pictures next to the table and give your toddler a card or two each time she's being changed. This usually keeps our baby happy. Cards with pictures of animals work best—you can get these at your local zoo.

Bill Adler, Jr.
Washington, D.C.

To get our 16-month-old to lie still during changes, I make sure she has a goal to focus on. There's a small shelf above the changing table just barely within her reach. I put a favorite stuffed animal up there and she occupies herself by trying to grab it while I change her.

Mary Donnelly
Brooklyn, New York

Does your toddler like to kick while on the changing table? Just take your toddler's feet in your hands and windmill her legs for a moment: Once she sees that you *want* to do this, she'll stop and quiet down.

Sally Danforth
Washington, D.C.

I had a little bowl of "special things" on a shelf near the changing table which my restless child could look at while having his diaper changed. They weren't toys but unusual and odd things like a spoon carved from bone (brought back from Wales) and some seashells. They were only to be examined when he was on the changing table and were left in the diapering area.

Terry Clifford
Takoma Park, Maryland

Sometimes, but certainly not always, we get David to keep still on the changing table by giving him his favorite book. He'll lie there and read, as if he's sitting on the toilet!

Regis Palmer
Berkeley, California

Sometimes it's nearly impossible to pick up your toddler to get her onto the changing table. Mention the word *diaper* and she curls up into an unmovable ball. But when I'm in a sneaky mood I ask Karen, "Where's your hair?" She immediately responds by putting both hands on top of her head, making it a cinch to pick her up. The same trick works for getting Karen out of the bath when she's disinclined.

Bill Adler, Jr.
Washington, D.C.

When my babies resisted having their diapers changed, I would often engage them in a game of identifying body parts. The litany can be endless, from "Where's your nose? Where's your eyes? Where's your ears?" to the harder parts like "Where's your elbow? Where's your knee?" It didn't work all the time, but often enough. I can remember one of the kids lying there, obviously thinking very hard, "Now, what the heck is an elbow?"

Ellen Peters
Springfield, Illinois

One great, distracting toy for the changing table is a new diaper. Toddlers are fascinated by their shape and texture.

Kathy Lewis
Middletown, New York

Every baby gets fussy on the diaper table. A technique I've found that
works with a baby who's reluctant to get on the table is to whirl him
around in your arms for a minute or two beforehand. This makes the
baby smile and temporarily puts him in a passive mode. Just be sure to
do the twirling *before* you take off the diaper.

Bill Adler, Jr.
Washington, D.C.

I use cloth diapers but find that double diapers are too bulky for the
baby. So I buy several packs of washcloths and fold one into the middle
of the cloth diaper when I want more protection. They are very
absorbent and are the perfect size.

Janet Elbaghetti
Takoma Park, Maryland

To save money when using disposable diapers, use the generic ones
during the day (when it doesn't matter much if they tear or leak), and
use the name-brand ones at night for better protection.

Marty Gregg
Webster Groves, Missouri

I used cloth diapers and found a shortcut to eliminating the most
distasteful part—wringing out the diapers in the water-filled diaper
pail when it was time to wash them. I just poured the full diaper pail
into the washer, letting the water drain out through the washing
machine. Then I would run the load through the usual wash with
detergent and bleach.

Jan Paul
Webster Groves, Missouri

I never had a changing table, but I bought one of those Rubbermaid
carry-alls—two rectangular boxes joined together with a sturdy handle
in the middle. I put diapers in one side and all the changing
paraphernalia (lotions, wipes, powder) in the other side. This was
handy and portable, and particularly helpful when our babies were
sleeping in our room and needed changing during the night.

Lisa Reutzloff
St. Ann, Missouri

Don't buy one of those fancy warmers for wipes. Just keep the container on top of the cable TV box. The wipes will stay warm because the cable box is constantly warm.

Nancy Nathan
Bethesda, Maryland

I don't have time to let Matthew "air out" every time I change his diaper (who can stand at the changing table for five minutes every time?), but Matthew was not getting enough air on his lower parts and small reddish areas were developing. Now, when I nurse him every morning, I leave him diaperless on a waterproof pad on the bed and put a cloth diaper lightly over the top of him—for obvious reasons. He always has a good 20 minutes to kick his legs and get plenty of air down under. The redness has now disappeared completely.

Cynthia Johnson
Forestville, Maryland

If the baby has diaper rash, give her a little sitz bath after every diaper change. Put about two tablespoons of baking soda into a sink full of lukewarm to cool water. Let her air dry, then apply ointment.

Cathy Shirski
Boston, Massachusetts

Ronnie had a diaper rash that just wouldn't go away. The doctor kept recommending lotions, but they only helped a little. The cure for us was frequent diaper changes—I mean really frequent, at least once every two hours during the day. Every time he smells the least bit poopy, I change him immediately, even if I changed him just 10 minutes before. I've also made it a habit to change him before and after a nap. It's more work for me, but I have a happier baby since his bottom no longer bothers him.

Pat Griffin
Pittsburgh, Pennsylvania

Here's the only known application for those perfumed advertisements that appear in magazines: Clip them and drop them into the diaper pail—they make great deodorizers.

Bill Adler, Jr.
Washington, D.C.

How do you open a diaper can without passing out? Many drugstores sell antiodor drops for colostomy patients. The brand I use is called Banish. A couple of drops in the diaper can, and I have a clean-smelling baby's room.

Bill Adler, Jr.
Washington, D.C.

Try a generic brand of petroleum jelly on the baby's bottom instead of more expensive ointments. My son never had a problem with diaper rash once I switched.

Martha Dolan
Maplewood, Missouri

Eating Out

Remember when you were single and went out to a restaurant and the maitre d' deposited a family with a baby at the table next to yours? Now it's your turn. Go ahead, have as good a time as you possibly can, but remember: Leave a big tip. In this section parents share their experiences of eating out with a toddler.

The moment you arrive at a restaurant, ask for four extra spoons or extra straws. Give them to the baby one at a time. She'll enjoy waving them around, banging them, and even occasionally mimicking you eating with the spoon. As each spoon drops to the floor, give her a new one. If you think you're troubling the server with your request for extra spoons, believe me, you're not: The server would much rather give you more spoons than hear a baby shriek.

Amy Caldwell
Flagstaff, Arizona

Bring some paper and markers to distract your preschooler while waiting for your pizza to bake. She can practice "writing" the alphabet, or she can draw family portraits.

Susan Golant
Los Angeles, California

Amy was so fussy and squirmy in most restaurants that I felt terrible for the other patrons. But one day I took her to an outdoor cafe, and she was great. She could stay in her stroller instead of those uncomfortable restaurant high chairs, and she could watch the traffic. She didn't feel that she was in a dark and confining space. And even if she did cry a bit, she was no louder than the usual level of street noise on the busy avenue. Now I always pick outdoor cafes, and we both enjoy our meals.

Martha Lanier
Vienna, Virginia

Always have a bag with crayons, paper, and crackers or Cheerios to take to any restaurant. Make it a special bag just for eating-out occasions.

> *Patty Noonan*
> *Kirkwood, Missouri*

In restaurants, don't wait for a toddler to get fussy before taking action. Have a designated walker: After ordering your meal, one adult takes the little one out for a walk and returns only when the food has arrived. After eating, another adult takes the child while the rest of the party enjoys coffee or tea. Even if the dining group only consists of two adults who have to trade-off the walking responsibility, it makes the actual meal more pleasant for everyone.

> *Sarah Kaskie*
> *Orlando, Florida*

Want to take your toddler to a restaurant but are tired of the usual franchise or "family" restaurants that are child-friendly but less-than-gourmet in cuisine? Try a good restaurant with outdoor seating. Typical toddler noise and mess are more easily tolerated in less formal outdoor dining, and you'll probably find that your wiggly, impatient child behaves better if kept in the sun (don't forget to bring sunscreen) instead of a dark, noisy, crowded indoor space.

> *Jane Olivieri*
> *Chicago, Illinois*

Rather than carry bibs to restaurants, I always carry a few of those little plastic hair clips in my purse so I can fasten a napkin around the baby's neck to make a bib.

> *Jeanne LaBella*
> *Arlington, Virginia*

Nobody has fond memories of dining out with toddlers. You can make the best of having to eat out by choosing a restaurant that is child-friendly (having high chairs and a children's menu is the least you should expect). A cassette player with a headset often occupies our four-year-old until the food comes. Don't linger over coffee and dessert.

Martha Shirk
Webster Groves, Missouri

We have a steadfast rule for fast-food restaurants: You can't eat any french fries until the hamburgers or nuggets (or whatever) are finished.

Anne O'Brien
Sandusky, Ohio

We always insisted on acceptable behavior in restaurants and told Julia that if her behavior was not acceptable, we would leave. She loved eating out, and it only took one time when we actually got up and walked out for her to learn that we meant it.

Bobbie Tate
Takoma Park, Maryland

Just because a favorite restaurant of yours doesn't have carry-out or delivery, this doesn't mean they can't or won't accommodate you. Restaurants want more business, not less, so if you ask them about a carry-out or delivery service you may be pleasantly surprised.

Bill Adler, Jr.
Washington, D.C.

When we go out to eat we always bring our own high-chair cushion along. The typical wooden high chairs in restaurants are hard and uncomfortable for little bottoms to sit on for long. Besides, the seats are often stained and gummy. Our child always sits quietly when he's on his familiar cushion.

Julie Ropier
Alexandria, Virginia

I pack a light cotton receiving blanket in my diaper bag and use it as a seat cover for restaurant high chairs, which are sometimes a bit grimy from the spills of the last hundred occupants. Also, that way I don't have to worry so much if the previous user had the flu.

Norma Klein
Teaneck, New Jersey

Here are some foods I've discovered are good to order for a baby when eating out:
• mashed potatoes
• spaghetti with *butter* sauce, not tomato sauce
• salted scrambled eggs
• applesauce
• cottage cheese
• creamed spinach
• creamed corn
• bread, toast, rolls, garlic bread, and bagels
• hot dogs (cut them into very small pieces and test their temperature)
• most soups (also test their temperature)
• crackers
Many restaurants will prepare these foods for you even if they're not on the menu.

Karen Razi
Cincinnati, Ohio

The best kiddie food for eating at nice restaurants is pasta without any sauce. The kids can really get into it without much mess on their nice clothes or on the table.

Renee Schuetter
Kailua, Hawaii

Get carry-out!

Sandra Fletcher
Silver Spring, Maryland

Feeding Time

There is no way to have a clean kitchen and a baby at the same time. That is, not unless you have round-the-clock help. With a baby, the kitchen becomes a multipurpose room: feeding chamber, play area, cooking center or place from which Pizza Hut is called), infant bath, sterilizing chamber for bottles and nipples, medicine dispensary, and, if you're lucky, the room in which you get to read the morning paper.

One thing is for certain: Food goes out a lot easier than it comes in. Why babies develop preferences for particular foods is a mystery. But better a mystery than a misery. Don't let your toddler's eating habits cause you despair. Go with the flow. Let your little one develop her own eating habits, rather than imposing your own preferences on her. Read on for more helpful hints.

Peel a whole apple, then core it with an apple corer, the kind that leaves a hole through the center. Baby can grasp the slippery, peeled apple by putting her fingers in the hole and eating around the sides.

Carmen D'Angelo
Brooklyn, New York

We've tried (and been pretty successful at) keeping our children from craving junk food all day. We never serve ice cream, only frozen yogurt. When they want a snack, we give them carrot sticks and apples instead of cookies. When they want something sweet, instead of candy they get raisins, grapes, bananas, or strawberries.

Elizabeth Dear
Falls Church, Virginia

Our son, Max, isn't a great milk drinker, so we make sure he gets calcium by feeding him yogurt, cottage cheese, and ice cream—especially ice cream.

> *Al Grice*
> *Gainesville, Florida*

It didn't last forever, but for a long time, Patrick and Bonnie thought that cookies were those little shredded wheats with fruit in the middle.

> *David Carlson*
> *Alexandria, Virginia*

When Kevin was an infant, I strictly adhered to the rule about not feeding your baby solid food until he or she is six months of age. He was a difficult baby, but the minute he started eating, he was happier. I would have started him on cereal much earlier if I had realized how hungry he was!

> *Rose Krasnow*
> *Rockville, Maryland*

When introducing new foods to baby, put a little bit of an already acceptable food on the end of the spoon—like a tiny amount of applesauce in front of the spinach.

> *Trish Cody*
> *Austin, Texas*

Christina is just learning to eat baby food. I put a little rice cereal on the spoon, but she doesn't know she's supposed to open her mouth. She has a musical peek-a-boo bear toy she always likes to put in her mouth, so I hold up the bear as if I'm going to give it to her. She opens her mouth for it, and then I pop in a spoonful of rice cereal, which she swallows quickly, so she can get her mouth open again to try to catch that peek-a-boo bear.

> *Meg Larsen*
> *Washington, D.C.*

A little preparation can ease the introduction of solids into a baby's diet. Day one: I let my baby play with the empty spoon, just so she could get the feel of it in her mouth so that it wouldn't be a strange object when I later filled it with food. Day two: I fed her expressed breast milk by spoon so that the taste of the first food she received by spoon would be familiar. Day three: I mixed a tiny amount of rice cereal into the expressed breast milk, not enough for her to notice anything different about the taste. Day four and onward: I gradually increased the ratio of cereal to breast milk so that by the end of the second week my baby was happily eating a small bowl of rice cereal (soon to be followed by oatmeal and other cereals, and later fruits, vegetables, and meats).

Joanna Johnson
Norwalk, Connecticut

Pique a young one's interest in a new food by announcing that it is for grown-ups only. He can have anything else on the table except the forbidden dish. Any kid old enough to talk will probably try to convince the cook that he should be allowed to try the new dish.

Maggie Keely Foley
Kirkwood, Missouri

If your toddler suddenly seems to love a particular food—say processed, sliced turkey—*don't* go out and buy a year's supply. Tomorrow your child could just as easily decide he doesn't care for that meal at all.

Bill Adler, Jr.
Washington, D.C.

For finger foods, give the baby frozen corn, peas, and carrots. These are easy to pick up and babies seem to like them even better when they are cold (they thaw so quickly that they are not really frozen when the kids eat them). Also, you can buy a single bag of mixed vegetables and store the bag in the freezer, taking out only as many as you need at one meal.

Kathy Ladd
St. Louis, Missouri

When making peanut butter and jelly sandwiches for lunches or picnics, put peanut butter on both slices of bread—not just one—and put the jelly in between. This sort of seals the jelly in and prevents the bread from getting soggy.

Nancy Foulkes
St. Louis, Missouri

Mix the peanut butter and jelly ahead of time—this way you get no jelly drips.

Susan Robinson
St. Louis, Missouri

When my husband and I were going out for dinner by ourselves and I didn't want to make the kids a whole meal, I would fix them a "fun supper" that consisted of four or five of these items: cubes of cheese, piles of raisins, slices of apple (sometimes spread with peanut butter), carrot sticks, piles of Cheerios, and so on. When they were a little older, I gave them each a toothpick to eat their fun supper with. Besides, it took a little longer for them to eat, giving us more time to get ready to go.

Jo Hoge
Takoma Park, Maryland

I often use cookie cutters to make sandwiches for the kids; it always makes the food more appealing when the cheese sandwich is shaped like a dinosaur or the peanut butter and jelly sandwich is shaped like a teddy bear. Freeze the leftover scraps of bread for the next trip to the duck pond.

Patricia Farrell
Torrance, California

When the kids start getting picky about what they will eat, it's time to get them involved in preparing the food. For some reason, the food tastes better when *they* make it. Some of our family favorites include ants on a log (peanut butter spread on celery with raisins on top), carrot coins (sliced carrots served with peanut butter), and shishkabob (fruit and cheese slices speared on plastic straws).

Kim Manning
Atlanta, Georgia

Buy snow cones *without* the syrup. Kids love the shaved ice and don't need the sweet syrup. This is also great for teething babies.

Patty Noonan
Kirkwood, Missouri

To avoid having to clean the floor under the high chair, put a small, rigid plastic wading pool underneath. After every meal, just dump the pool.

Terry Lean
Mercerville, Indiana

I had always heard that babies prefer bland food. We have a very picky eater, and he hardly touched any baby foods that came in jars. We finally discovered why—they were just too bland for him. He would only eat foods with a really strong taste: guacamole, garlic bread, spicy Chinese noodles, empanadas (Mexican meat pies). Now he eats pretty well, though he sometimes does have pungent baby breath.

Sandy Lessor
Ann Arbor, Michigan

For picky eaters who don't eat enough vegetables and fruits, chop up the unacceptable foods and put them in homemade muffins. Most kids like muffins.

Marty Gregg
Webster Groves, Missouri

On a lazy day, when I can't get my two boys to focus on lunch, I tell them a story. Every time I use the word *baseball*, they must take a bite of food. Since it's a game, they go for it. No giggling is allowed because I tell them that eating is serious business. When the food's gone, the story ends.

Sally Tippett Rains
St. Louis, Missouri

When feeding messy toddlers, a plastic shower curtain cut in half protects the floor under the high chair and makes for easy cleaning.

Jan Paul
Webster Groves, Missouri

When John was about two years old, we pretended that his food talked to him—particularly the vegetables. The food would beg him to eat them—he always liked the game.

Renee Schuetter
Kailua, Hawaii

If your baby is a light eater, try this: Give her a piece of fruit that she likes—say a peeled apple or pear. When she picks it up in one hand and starts to eat it, give her a second slice to hold in the other hand. She really will eat twice as much that way. This trick works nearly every time with Sara.

Max Herman
Fairbanks, Alaska

Try this with your finicky eater: Remove the high-chair tray and pull the high chair directly up to the table so that you can feed the baby bits of mashed food from your own plate. We did this with Susie and it worked like a dream. She seemed to prefer food that came from our plates rather than from her own. Besides, adult food is tastier than bland baby food.

Millie Walters
Bangor, Maine

Karen was a problem eater. Basically the problem was that she didn't like to eat. Then one week she had diarrhea, and the pediatrician advised giving her half formula, half water. Three days later when we reintroduced solid food, she was ravenous and ate like a tiger. Since then we've continued to dilute her formula with water, and Karen has continued to amaze us by eating just about everything we put in front of her. Today she ate a grilled-cheese sandwich! Check with your pediatrician before trying this.

Bill Adler, Jr.
Washington, D.C.

We've done this since Lily was about 15 months old: When she resists eating a particular food, my husband almost always gets her to eat it by saying dramatically, "Don't eat that! No, don't do *that!*" When Lily was a baby, she ate it triumphantly. Now that she's four, it's more of a joke. But it still works!

Margaret Edelman
Garden City, New York

I always made my own baby food—it was cheaper and I knew exactly what the baby was eating. I would use my Cuisinart to puree carrots or other vegetables and then freeze them in ice cube trays. I also used a baby food grinder to grind up meat, which would then also be frozen. You only need to pop out as many cubes of food as you need and microwave them. When we were going out, I'd put some cubes in old baby food jars, and by the time dinner rolled around, they would usually be thawed out.

Elaine Anderson
Hastings, Nebraska

When they're very young, teach your children to clear their own plates, utensils, and cups from the table. This should be a lifelong habit, and three years of age is not too early to learn it.

Becky Hagen
Portland, Oregon

Here's how I got the baby to enjoy having her face wiped after eating.
First I taught her how to make a funny "b-b-b-b" noise by strumming
her lower lip with her finger. When I want to wipe her face I start
strumming her lip with my own finger, then I quickly substitute a
damp paper towel and continue to strum her mouth. She thinks the
game is still going on and happily continues making her noise while
I wipe.

Elizabeth Prungel
Huntington Valley,
Pennsylvania

To clean a baby's face after eating, wet a washcloth and give it to your
baby. As he plays with it, he'll clean off his hands and face all by
himself!

Ann Dunn
Manchester,
New Hampshire

Always keep one of those plastic ice scrapers handy in the kitchen.
They remove almost anything from hard surfaces without scratching
the surface, including dried baby cereal, old dough, even hardened
drops of pancake batter.

Anne Morrison
Lansing, Michigan

The difficult part about solid-food feeding is getting the stuff off the
baby's hands and face after you're done. My daughter cries every time I
get near her with a towel, so my husband started cleaning her by
putting her hands under the warm running water of the kitchen faucet.
He freely splashes the water up to her mouth and gently rubs her face
with his hand. At first I thought this was strange, but she loves it and
smiles and shrieks for more. And she doesn't even mind being dried
with the towel afterward.

Janet Douglas
Takoma Park, Maryland

There's an electric outlet on the wall behind the baby's high chair, and it's the perfect place to plug in a hand-held vacuum cleaner like a Dustbuster or Mini-Vac. Now, chasing down stray zwieback crumbs or escaped Cheerios is fast and easy.

Joel Ehrlich
New Haven, Connecticut

Need a few more large bibs? Just take some old dish towels or hand towels, wrap them around the baby, mark them with chalk where they come together at the back, and stick some Velcro dots on to make the closing. You can buy adhesive-backed Velcro dots, iron-ons, or sew-ons. If you're doing iron-ons, buy some iron-on letters at the same time and spell your baby's name on the bib.

VELCRO DOTS

SAM

AM

CHALK MARK

Laura McAdoo
Indianapolis,
Indiana

We introduced our baby to cup drinking in the tub. It didn't matter how much of the water she spilled, and we made sure she didn't drink the bathwater.

Peggy Robin
Washington, D.C.

If your child gets most of her food on her clothing rather than the bib, don't bother to use a bib. That way you'll have one less thing to wash.

Bill Adler, Jr.
Washington, D.C.

Furniture

With a new baby, for the first few weeks all you need is a bassinet and changing table. In fact, you may not even need a changing table, because newborns don't care what kind of surface they're changed on. But soon you'll be acquiring all sorts of furniture—not just a crib and dresser, but little chairs and tables, too. Your crib will have a mattress, a dust ruffle, a rubber sheet, a main sheet, a crib bib or other cover to keep various liquids from reaching the main sheet, a blanket, assorted stuffed animals—so many layers that you may never see the beautiful, expensive sheet you purchased long before! The following responses reveal what other parents have learned when it comes to combining furniture and children.

Buy one of the wooden changing tables that can be used as a bookshelf when the baby is older.

Nancy Nathan
Bethesda, Maryland

We used a wooden port-a-crib for our changing table. The thin pad can be adjusted to three levels. Most of the time, it was adjusted to the top level to be used as a changing table, but occasionally—for guests or special outdoor events—we used it as a crib or playpen. Also, we had several sheets in the port-a-crib size, so instead of washing the changing-table pad, we simply changed the sheets.

Eileen Keevan
Hammond, Indiana

Those gliding lounge chairs are better than wooden rocking chairs—particularly when feeding infants.

Various parents

Don't waste your money on high-priced bassinets and fancy bathing equipment for infants. They will be too big for that stuff by the time they are two months old. Invest your money in solid equipment that your kids are going to use for a long time: the crib, car seat, and high chair.

Tim O'Neill
St. Louis, Missouri

Buy an old card table at a garage sale and cut the legs off to the height at which your toddler or young child can use it. When it's not in use, fold it up and put it away!

Mary Westerman
St. Louis, Missouri

I didn't want to spend the money for a changing table when I already had a three-drawer dresser with a wide, flat top about the right height for changing diapers. I made a changing surface by laying down a piece of foam cut to the right dimensions and covering it with a piece of quilted vinyl I bought in the upholstery section of a fabric store. I nailed the vinyl-covered foam to the edges of the dresser top with carpet tacks. Just to make sure that the heads of the tacks couldn't pop back up and snag the baby, I covered them with bright vinyl tape. To make the dresser fit the decor of the baby's room, I painted it sky blue with nontoxic paint. On the upper two drawers I painted fluffy white clouds. On the bottom drawer I painted a green-blue sea and a little red sailboat with a yellow flag flying from its mast. Our little boy loves his seascape dresser/changing table.

Burt Fisher
Charleston,
South Carolina

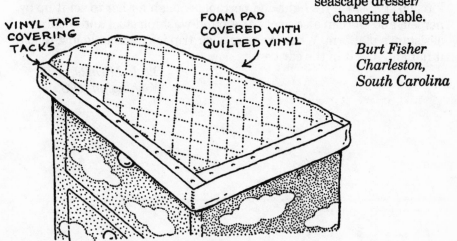

VINYL TAPE
COVERING
TACKS

FOAM PAD
COVERED WITH
QUILTED VINYL

We have a high chair that's mostly plastic and vinyl. It's not as
attractive as a wooden one, but it's so much easier to clean. I discovered
that you can detach the tray and pop it in the dishwasher. When the
chair is really covered with goo, take it outside and hose it down.
Periodically, when you're washing the car, put the high chair in the
driveway and give it a good blast of soapy water, followed by a rinse.
The plastic parts dry very quickly in the sun, and the high chair looks
like new.

Kimberly Hancock
Park Forest, Illinois

Buy a crib that is solid on at least one end so that when you tiptoe in to
check on the baby, he doesn't see you.

Donna Brennan
Silver Spring, Maryland

You don't need to buy bassinet sheets. Standard pillow cases work fine.
Just tuck them under the bassinet mattress at the foot.

Martha Jaffe
Kensington, Maryland

My daughter thinks she's too big for a high chair, but we think she's not
quite big enough to sit on the regular chairs around our kitchen table.
We've found what seems to be the perfect in-between chair for her: a
kitchen step-stool. It's light and portable enough for her to set it up by
herself, and she can also use it as a hand-washing stool and cooking
assistant's platform. When we take a car trip it's no trouble just to fold
it flat and toss it in the car trunk.

Dia L. Michels
Washington, D.C.

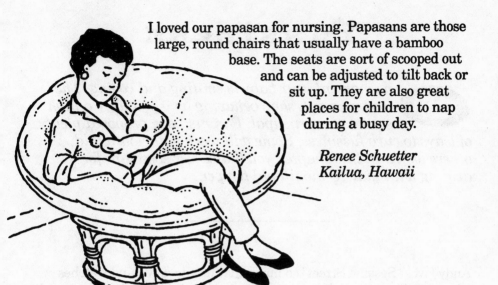

I loved our papasan for nursing. Papasans are those large, round chairs that usually have a bamboo base. The seats are sort of scooped out and can be adjusted to tilt back or sit up. They are also great places for children to nap during a busy day.

Renee Schuetter
Kailua, Hawaii

Fussiness

One moment your baby is smiling and cooing. The next moment, she's behaving as if you were a high school vice principal. Parents have proposed plenty of ways to curb fussiness. Some will work with your child, others won't. In this chapter, you'll discover some tips for dealing with that 18-month-old temper.

Andy loves "Sesame Street" so much that he sits down and watches whenever it's on, even if he's been fussy only minutes before. We taped some of the best episodes and now, when he seems to be at loose ends, we play a tape for him. Hearing "Sunny day, sweeping the clouds away..." is a lot better than listening to screams all day.

Candy Dermott
Racine, Wisconsin

When my 16-month-old is fussy on the changing table, I make a funny face at her—sort of a quizzical I-know-what-you're-doing look. I don't know why, but it usually makes her stop fidgeting and kicking.

Bill Adler, Jr.
Washington, D.C.

I have a difficult-to-dress wiggler, James. I used to try to hold him on the changing table and struggle with his clothes. Now I just put James down on the floor in his diaper and let him come over to the drawers and "help" me pick out his clothes. He loves to pull out shirts and pants and hand them to me. I still have to try to corral him to get him dressed, but at least he's not yelling and crying anymore as I make the attempt.

Christine Yall
Front Royal, Virginia

Ever have trouble getting your toddler to follow you as you're walking on the sidewalk? You know the problem: You are trying to get home, but your child is interested in the pile of pebbles she's spotted. Try this. Stand about 30 feet away from your toddler in the direction you want to go. Spread your legs and yell, "Under the bridge!" Your child will come running between your legs. Keep this up till you get home. This trick works fastest with two parents.

Bill Adler, Jr. &
Peggy Robin
Washington, D.C.

When the baby can't settle down, I use one of those back rests for myself and let him lie on my chest. He can hear my heartbeat and is usually comforted, and I get some semblance of rest.

Jeanne LaBella
Alexandria, Virginia

This sounds weird, but it really worked. When the baby was screaming his head off and I couldn't comfort him, I would start vacuuming. It would quiet him instantly, and usually by the time I finished vacuuming, he would be asleep. I get a clean house and a quiet baby at the same time.

Jill Woo
Silver Spring, Maryland

After going through the evening fussies with a fourth baby, I've become a true believer in swaying and dancing with the baby to music. Each baby seems to have his own taste. One baby loved rock music—the Beatles and the Rolling Stones, but definitely *not* the Doors. The latest baby loves classical music, especially Mozart.

Maria Childress
St. Louis, Missouri

Ditto to the above. Unfortunately, Grace likes polka music.

Jim Mosley
Affton, Missouri

If your child loves particular cartoon characters—Winnie the Pooh, the Little Mermaid, or Teenage Mutant Ninja Turtles—use that to your advantage. Claim to know for a fact that the Little Mermaid eats all her vegetables or that Michelangelo always goes to bed promptly at 8:30. Your child will also be impressed that you are so familiar with the habits and preferences of his favorite characters.

Donna Kelly
Cleveland, Ohio

Spinning a toddler around until you can no longer spin can often turn a fussy child into a happy one.

Judith Allen
North Conway,
New Hampshire

If your toddler is chilly in the morning, *don't* put a jacket on him. We did that one morning, and as soon as we put a jacket on Steve, he demanded to go "out."

Nan Farrell
Andover, Massachusetts

When your child is old enough not to put everything you give her in her mouth, a good diverting activity is to let her look through unwanted mail-order catalogs. It's like getting new picture books all the time. Our 20-month-old especially loves the baby product and toy catalogs. Carrie will sit looking at pictures of other kids and toys for 10 minutes at a time—an eternity in babydom.

Barbara Halperin
Madison, Wisconsin

One simple way to divert a baby or (sometimes) a toddler: Make a few fun noises. Blow into an empty soda bottle, squish water in your hands, talk into a hollow tube or can, run a moist finger across the rim of a crystal glass, or make popping noises with your thumb and mouth.

Candy Albright
Leesburg, Virginia

Grandparents and Other Relations

Why is it that grandparents are never around when you simply want to go out to dinner alone with your spouse, but they always manage to drop by when the baby is taking a nap? Read on for some ideas on how to transform your own parents into grandparents.

Once your baby is crawling or walking, you'll want to make sure your parents' house is at least a little babyproof before you visit. Give your parents a checklist of hazards to watch out for. For their own sake, have them remove valuable and breakable objects from baby's reach. Provide them with covers for electrical outlets, and by all means make sure they get a stair barrier. If they live in a high rise, make sure the windows are closed and locked.

Kitty Nelson
Bethesda, Maryland

A common parents' complaint is that the grandparents refuse to do things the parents' way. They gave *you* solid food at three months and *you* grew up fine, so why do you refuse to let them try to feed your five-month-old a little mashed banana? If they won't accept your child-rearing practices, they may respect the words of a well-known authority. Find articles or passages from baby-care books that back up what you're doing and send them to your parents.

Lucy Albright
Baltimore, Maryland

When visiting, be sure to take along some of your child's familiar toys
from home. Being in an unfamiliar place, even with many new things
to explore, can be overwhelming to some kids, especially when
confronted with excited grandparents. It's comforting to have some of
the things from home.

Betsy Wilkson
Duluth, Minnesota

To keep your toddler familiar with the faces of grandparents who live
far away and visit only a few times a year, make a videotape of the
grandparents saying hello to your baby and telling a story or singing a
song. Show it to your child fairly often so that when the grandparents
do visit she won't be scared or shy.

Debbie McKenna
Meriden, Connecticut

I use the computer to make "Matthew-grams" for grandparents and
other relatives to keep them updated on Matthew's latest
developments. The newsletter format includes "crib notes" (anecdotes
about what he's been up to) and usually a few columns on Mom and
Dad. I am also able to scan in a few photos. It's a great way to keep in
touch with everyone.

Steve Johnson
Forestville, Maryland

The grandparents *will* do things differently from you—everyone has his
or her own style of child care. But *relax*. Don't draw lines in the
sandbox over little things. Children learn quickly that just because
Grandma gives them a piece of candy after dinner at *her* house, that
doesn't mean they will get the same treatment at home. As long as
grandparents are loving (and there are no obvious safety problems),
you should allow your parents a little leeway with their grandchildren.

Sarah Kaskie
Orlando, Florida

Grandparents don't need to spend money on a big crib and high chairs.
They can buy good, lightweight, portable cribs that double as playpens.
You'll also find strap-on chair-and-tray sets that convert almost any
dining room chair into a high chair.

Laura Dunn
Elizabeth, New Jersey

We never hesitate to call out-of-town grandparents after any notable
event, whether it's the first day of preschool, the annual dance recital,
the first soccer game, whatever. As far as we're concerned, money spent
on phone calls between children and grandparents is money well spent.

Veronica Campbell
Chesterfield, Missouri

When Grandma babysits, write down the baby's schedule—when he
had his last bottle, when he gets his solid foods, when he will need a
nap, and so on. It helps for grandparents to *know* the schedule, even if
they don't stick to it all the time.

"Grandma"
Marie Schiller
St. Louis, Missouri

Since all of our relatives live out of town, I have made a special book for
my daughter just of grandparents, aunts, uncles, and cousins. It's *her*
photo album. We often look at it together and I tell her over and over
who the family members are. Also, I try to include lots of pictures of her
with the various relatives.

Kim Manning
Atlanta, Georgia

Grandparents might feel more secure when your child stays over if
they designate one or two rooms as baby-safe areas and *thoroughly*
childproof those spaces.

Nancy Chew
Woodstock, New York

I was worried that something might happen to Chris, my two-year-old, while she was visiting her grandparents. I knew that I couldn't get my parents to take a CPR [cardiopulmonary resuscitation] class like my wife and I did (they don't even wear their seat belts in cars). So I bought a baby first-aid video and had them watch it. It's not a complete course in baby CPR, but at least they won't be completely lost in an emergency.

Harold Wains
St. Louis, Missouri

Grooming

There's no reason why a baby can't look nice. (Of course, they always look wonderful to you.) A trim of the bangs and fingernails here, a wipe of the mouth there, and voilà, a brand-new, ready-to-show-off baby. Except for one thing: Babies don't always want to cooperate. As you'll see in the following pages, in this contest of parent versus baby, sometimes we parents win, and sometimes we lose.

Most new parents are nervous about cutting their baby's nails. They should be! I nicked my baby's finger with one of those supposedly blunt baby nail scissors. After that I never cut, I only file. I use a nail file made especially for baby's soft fingernails.

Lorraine Kuyper
Washington, D.C.

Cut baby's nails while she's in the bath—that's when nails are softest.

Carol Watkins
Glens Falls, New York

I did most of Ronnie's nail-trimming when he was nursing. He was so intent on getting his milk, he hardly noticed what I was up to with his fingers.

Heather Harris
Alexandria, Virginia

I cut Sally's nails when she's asleep in the car seat and the car's stopped at a light. I only get one or two nails per light, but I start with the sharpest ones first.

Cynthia Alberts
New York, New York

Making up little verbal routines is helpful. Instead of saying "I'm going to cut your fingernails tonight," I say "It's nail night," like it's something special. Or I say "It's hair night" when it's time to shampoo. Small children respond as if it's part of the calendar rather than your seemingly arbitrary decision to cut their nails.

Marianne Alweiss
New York, New York

I suggest cutting nails while your baby is in a feeding seat and distracted with a bottle or sipper cup. One parent holds the bottle for the baby while the other trims away.

Dave Jones
McLean, Virginia

I set aside a regular time after the bath to deal with Roy's nails and clean his baby teeth with a gauze pad. His nails are usually softer after some time in the tub, and he has gotten used to letting me tend to his hands and mouth right after I've cleaned the rest of him.

Kim Donnelly
Livingston, New Jersey

I cut Allie's fingernails when she is fast asleep.

Diane Kantor
Scarsdale, New York

I bought a double-sided toddler's toothbrush to do Laurie's teeth. It takes half the time that way.

Laura Dupree
New York, New York

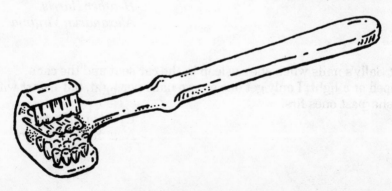

When I'm giving my kids a haircut and it's time to cut the bangs, I ask them to look up at my face and then I ask questions like "What color are Mommy's eyes?" "How many freckles does Mommy have?" "Can you stare at my eyes without blinking?"

They usually have to concentrate long enough for me to finish the hard task of cutting bangs.

Dot Starek
Hillsboro, Missouri

Until your child is old enough to want a particular type of hairstyle, don't bother with professional hair cutters. Most toddlers are frightened of a stranger manipulating their heads. If you're steady enough to cut a straight line, you can trim bangs to keep the hair out of your child's eyes.

Peggy Robin
Washington, D.C.

Use a baby nail scissors with rounded ends to trim your baby's hair. That reduces the danger of nicking your baby's skin with the tip of the scissors.

Noelle Spain
Falls Church, Virginia

When it's haircut time, I pack up my child's favorite books and a favorite snack to take to the shop. I hold the child on my lap and read while the stylist quickly does what she can in the shortest amount of time.

Anne Morrison
Lansing, Michigan

When it's time for haircuts, we set up a play beauty parlor with me pretending to be the stylist. We start with my asking who has the first appointment. I also cut my daughters' fingernails and give them "manicures." With four little girls, this is a big hit.

Sandy Egan
Princeton, New Jersey

Ask the barber to cut your baby's hair dry, not wet. Toddlers are frightened to be bent backward over a shampoo basin and doused.

Alice Winter
Reno, Nevada

To remove gum from hair I was told to use peanut butter. It works and also makes everyone laugh.

Toni Moras
Anchorage, Alaska

Health and Medicine

All babies get sick—colds, fevers, earaches, stomachaches, all sorts of maladies. The information in this chapter doesn't necessarily tell you how to cure a sick child, but it does tell you how to keep your child happy and reasonably pain-free until the illness passes.

Antibiotics taken for impetigo or ear infections can often cause a yeasty diaper rash. You can prevent this by applying a protective diaper ointment at every change, starting immediately after your baby has taken the first dose of medicine. Giving your baby lots of yogurt—with active cultures, not baby yogurt—can also help counteract the tendency to get a rash by restoring the balance between bacteria and yeast.

Nancy Donworth
Montreal, Quebec,
Canada

When Cara has diarrhea, I add a couple of drops of Lactaid to her milk. The Lactaid reduces the lactic sugar in the milk, and it's this sugar that aggravates the diarrhea. Less lactic sugar, less diarrhea.

Sandy Simon
Salem, Massachusetts

Band-Aids are limitless in our house. If a Band-Aid helps my kids feel better, they can have one whenever they want it—even for those microscopic "hurts" that are almost invisible to the human eye.

Terry Clifford
Takoma Park, Maryland

We got our son a Hasbro Checkup Center. It comes with toy shots, an X-ray machine, blood-pressure cuff, and stethoscope. We used a Cabbage Patch doll to show him what the doctor does, and then we let him give his doll a checkup. The next time we took him to the doctor he actually seemed interested in what the doctor was doing rather than screaming his head off.

Marjorie O'Connell
Englewood, New Jersey

Cut Band-Aids in half lengthwise—they fit on children's fingers much better that way.

Diana Cohn
San Francisco,
California

We keep Cold Comfort on call in the freezer for whenever anyone gets a scrape or a hurt calling for ice. It's self-contained (no drippy mess from ice cubes and plastic bags), molds itself to the body, and is more comfortable than ice. Cold Comfort is found at most pharmacies and costs from $4 to $6.

Terry Clifford
Takoma Park, Maryland

I noticed my baby had a bumpy, red, ring-shaped rash, sometimes on her chest, sometimes on her back. My doctor recommended various creams and lotions, and we experimented with different soaps and bath oils—we even switched laundry detergents a few times—but the rashes kept coming back. Then I noticed that the red spots matched up very well with the snaps on her clothing. She got the spots on her back right after sleeping in pajamas that snapped up the back, and she got them on her chest after wearing playsuits with metal snaps down the front. I sewed a strip of protective cotton over the part where the metal came into contact with her skin, and after that the rashes disappeared. Since I made this discovery, I've met three other parents whose babies had this same reaction, and in none of those cases did the doctor realize that metal snaps could cause the problem.

Bonnie Wilder
Albany, New York

For the baby who gets an ear infection every time he gets a cold, try having him sleep in a crib with his head elevated. Since you should not give a pillow to a child under age two, the best way is to insert a foam wedge underneath the fitted crib sheet or mattress so that one end is higher than the other. If your baby scoots in the other direction, just turn him around while he is fast asleep. A raised head does help to keep the ear canal free of fluids.

Scott King
Paterson, New Jersey

Whenever we have to give liquid medicine to Jennifer, we put it in a cordial glass rather than a spoon. It helps prevent spills, and she thinks it's a big deal to have it that way.

Diana Cohn
San Francisco,
California

The pediatrician said to give the baby a half teaspoon of medicine four times a day, but he didn't tell us how. We tried spoon feeding it to her, but she'd turn her head aside at the critical moment and the syrupy medicine would end up on her shirt. The baby medicine dropper we tried next worked a little better, but not by much. And mixing the medicine into her baby food was a complete disaster—in protest she refused to eat any solid food for days. One method, however, was moderately successful: We put the medicine in a syringe (without a needle, of course!), inserted it in her mouth toward the side, and quickly squirted in the dose. We learned not to squirt too far toward the back of her mouth so she wouldn't gag.

Susan Johns
Newark, New Jersey

To get Judy to take Tylenol drops, we had to try three different flavors until we found one she actually liked. (The first two came out as quickly as they went in.) Grape worked for us. Orange is what Judy's sister preferred. I recommend trying all flavors before you give up.

Sally Franks
Miami, Florida

To give Tylenol drops to your baby, add the correct dosage to a small amount of warm water in a bottle, and your baby will drink it like fruit juice.

Various parents

To combat "cradle cap" dermatitis on your baby's head, gently rub his scalp with a rough terry washcloth dabbed in mineral oil. The flakes will easily loosen and come off.

Daphne English
Madison, Wisconsin

I was afraid to take my baby's temperature because I worried about what would happen if she wiggled around and somehow broke the glass thermometer off while it was in her behind. Then I found a digital thermometer that's virtually unbreakable. It also has a safety stop on the end so it's impossible to hurt your baby by sticking it in too far. It only takes a minute, beeps when it's done, and records the last temperature taken, so the next time you turn the thermometer on, you're reminded what the previous reading was. The one I use is made by First Years, but there are other brands as well.

Cheryl Latinski
Cheverly, Maryland

I find the easiest, safest way to take my baby's temperature is by the underarm method (the child-care books call it axillary temperature). I don't have to take his diaper off, only his shirt. I lay him on his back (he's too young to sit up yet), put the thermometer in his armpit, use one hand to play with and hold his hands, and at the same time hold the thermometer steady until I have a reading. I always keep in mind that an underarm temperature will be a degree lower than an oral temperature and two degrees lower than a rectal temperature, and I make sure to tell my pediatrician how the temperature was taken when I call to tell her the results.

Barbara Patrick
Atlanta, Georgia

When Maxine, our one-year-old, is sick with a cold or has a mild fever we give her a warm bath. The bath, with all its bath toys, takes her mind off her runny nose. The moist air is good for her congestion and the tepid water is cool enough to bring down her temperature. We're careful to have a thick towel waiting to keep her from getting chilly before we get her clothes on.

Gabrielle Nagel
Long Island City,
New York

When I take my baby to the pediatrician's office I always bring along a receiving blanket and lay it down over the paper on the examining table. Benjamin tolerates the visit much better when he's lying on a soft, familiar blanket.

Barbara Franke
Chevy Chase, Maryland

When I took my son in for his checkup, I let the doctor examine me first to show him there was nothing to fear. The doctor tested my reflexes with his hammer and listened to my chest with the stethoscope before he tested my son's reflexes and listened to his chest. Seeing me smile through the examination helped to reassure my son, and having the stethoscope on my chest first helped to warm it up a little for his comfort, too.

Janna Rosenbaum
Concord, California

When learning to walk, bumped foreheads are so common that it's worthwhile to coax your baby to withstand the milder bumps without screaming. Try this: Every time the baby goes down, don't rush over and attempt to oversoothe him by saying, "Oh, did you hurt yourself?" (leading your child to expect to be hurt). Instead, just give him some hugs—that's usually more soothing anyway to a child who's screaming at the top of his lungs.

Sandy Kellner
Cincinnati, Ohio

Maintaining Parental Sanity

There's an unspoken competition among new parents: Which couple has gone the longest without having been to a restaurant or movie, or gone on a romantic vacation? Between the birth of your child and the chance to finally enjoy a night on the town, here are some ways to maintain your sanity and restore balance to your life.

The best thing I ever did with my baby was join a mother-and-child play group. It got me out of the house regularly and I got to know other adults. Our baby became used to playing with other children. We both learned a lot!

Janice Macoy
Warrenton, Virginia

With four kids all under eight, my husband and I often feel we're under siege by munchkins. To keep our sanity, we have given ourselves one place of refuge—our living room, which we have officially declared a child-free zone. It's one room in the house just for us, where we can keep nice, breakable things, don't have to babyproof (except for the gates that keep the kids out), and can entertain guests without having to do a massive clean-up first. All other rooms in the house—the kitchen, family room, bedrooms—can look like an explosion in a toy factory, but we don't mind because we know we can always escape to our adults-only room, put on a CD, and lose ourselves in our own world for a time.

Doris Wellstone
Denver, Colorado

Geoffrey's favorite toy is our telephone. It was constantly off the hook until we put a large rubber band over the small buttons on the receiver that indicate when the phone is on the hook. This way the phone is never off the hook, unless we move the rubber band to actually make a call. It won't work for every phone, but it does for ours.

Diana Cohn
San Francisco,
California

If you absolutely need to rest for a few minutes and your child is wide awake, play "beauty parlor." Stretch out on the bed or couch with your hair hanging over the side or arm; let your toddler or young child "style" your hair using combs, brushes, barrettes, and those old pink foam curlers. This is so relaxing and the minute they leave your side (or head, in this case), you know it and can attend to them.

Frances Noonan
Kirkwood, Missouri

When you want to do something uninterrupted (finish that chapter in the mystery novel, or talk on the telephone) try setting a task for your toddler that will take a while to complete. I take all the stuffed animals out of my toddler's toy box and line them up in the closet, then ask her to move them all back to their original house. She gets quite absorbed in the problem and makes numerous trips back and forth moving each animal, one at a time, while I have a chance to read, or make phone calls, or maybe just sit down and rest for a few minutes.

Lydia Lopez
Gainesville, Florida

When I don't feel like taking my 18-month-old someplace that he insists on going—for example, over to see the neighbor's pet bunny—I tell him that everyone is napping over there. He understands that and accepts it better than if I had simply said no, you can't go now.

Lisa Gentile
New Haven, Connecticut

If your toddler has a favorite book such as *Goodnight Moon*, memorize it. When he demands to be read to, you can recite it effortlessly without stopping whatever else you were doing. I've "read" *Goodnight Moon* many times to my son while continuing to do a crossword puzzle. I automatically know when to "turn" the pages, too.

> *Joan Johnstone*
> *Phoenix, Arizona*

My toddler loves to pull plants off tables and plant stands. I couldn't face getting rid of my wonderful greenery, so I moved all my plants into hanging pots and suspended them from hooks in the ceiling, far above my child's grabby reach.

> *Jennifer Tate*
> *Scarsdale, New York*

I used to joke that my perfume was "eau de vomit" and lost a few nice jackets and dresses to smelly milk stains until I finally bought an off-white wool scarf, which I threw over my shoulder when I wore "nice" clothes and carried the baby. It certainly looked better than always having a cloth diaper hanging over my shoulder when I'm out.

> *Patricia Farrell*
> *Torrance, California*

As the mother of twins, I strongly recommend that parents have babies one at a time.

> *Cathy Johnson*
> *Silver Spring, Maryland*

When you get home from the hospital with the baby, put a message on your answering machine that you are resting and will get back to your callers when you can. Keep it on whether or not you're resting. That way, you can return congratulatory calls at your leisure.

> *Ellen Peters*
> *Springfield, Illinois*

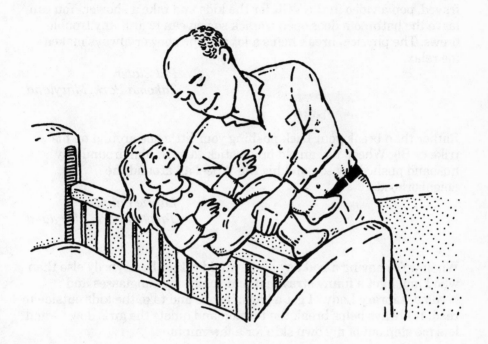

There's a simple but sad equation of parenting: Raising children produces lower back pain. Even the strongest succumb. I discovered that one way to avoid putting my back in agony every time I picked up or put down Karen was to lower her sideways. Every doctor tells you to bend at the knees to prevent back injury, but you can't do that when putting a toddler in a crib. So I turn at the hip. Now my back is back in great shape!

Bill Adler, Jr.
Washington, D.C.

When we were going through an extreme case of colic with our second child, it really helped me to have an agreed-on schedule with my husband for handling the screaming baby. I knew every night that I could hand the crying baby to Tom at 9 P.M. for his shift and go to bed knowing the baby would be well taken care of.

Terry Clifford
Takoma Park, Maryland

If you're having one of those days when your nerves are completely
frayed, pop a video in the VCR for the kids and take a shower. You can
leave the bathroom door open a crack so you can hear if any trouble
brews. The physical break helps a lot and the shower always makes
me relax.

Pat Slater
Takoma Park, Maryland

Rather than break your back pushing your little one around on his
trike or Big Wheel, use an old broomstick to push him around. My
husband pushed my son and his Big Wheel all around the
neighborhood.

Laurie Palmer
Takoma Park, Maryland

When we're having a bad day and I would rather be anybody else than
who I am, I get a funny straw hat and some silly sunglasses and
become "Library Lady." I get a bag of books and take the kids outside to
read. It always helps break the tension and quiets the girls down—and
lets me step out of my own skin for a few minutes.

Patty Bohn
Webster Groves, Missouri

I sometimes talk to my toddler using different funny voices that I have
invented for her stuffed animals. When Mr. Bear says that it's time to
go to the crib, she's often more willing to go than when Mommy says so.
She may even agree to try a new food if Quacky Duck tells her how
yummy it is first, and pretends to take a bite.

Sonia Rivkin
Los Angeles, California

Our neighborhood play group has been wonderful for me and my son.
We have five moms involved. The group meets two mornings a week for
two hours; two mothers stay to care for the children and the other three
are "off." On the sixth day of our three-week cycle, we all go on a
mini–field trip to a playground or someplace simple. The group has
provided a terrific introduction to socialization for my son and given me
needed companionship and relief.

Sandra Fletcher
Silver Spring, Maryland

I have a file called "Memories" on our home computer, and when I sit down at the computer, I often open that file and add a few things we have done recently or cute things the girls have said or done. It's basically a running log of their lives. Occasionally I get my calendar to help jog my thoughts about what we've done recently.

Laurie Potts-Dupre
College Park, Maryland

I maintain a baby book for each of my children, but to prevent myself from losing track of time between entries, I mark my calendar every three months with the words *write in baby book*. I also keep a piece of paper on the refrigerator to list things that I want to enter: first tooth, first words, funny expressions of speech. Having the list makes writing the actual entries simpler and faster.

Sandy Egan
Princeton, New Jersey

If you want to maintain friendships with other adults, be careful about the words you use around your toddler. From about a year and a half on, they become perfect mimics: Say the word *ugly* in front of little Jimmy, and little Jimmy will call your boss ugly when the boss comes over for dinner.

Callie Smith
Providence, Rhode Island

The key principle I apply to getting things done with a baby in the house: Never do anything while the baby is napping that could just as well be accomplished when she's awake. Save the precious nap time for those things that you really need to devote your full attention to. For example, make phone calls to friends and family—particularly those who have children—while your baby is up. Because they also have kids, they usually won't mind if the call is interrupted. Make important business calls only during naptime, and make them early in the nap. Fold laundry while your baby is up and sitting in a baby seat or playing nearby. Save sewing projects that require concentration (or sharp needles) for when your baby is asleep.

Carrie Donald
Ames, Iowa

Take up bicycling with a baby seat on the back. It's something you can
enjoy at your own level, and the kids really have fun, too.

Margie Frievogel
Bethesda, Maryland

Schedule your clean-up time at the same time every day and expect
everyone to participate from the toddler on up. We do our cleaning and
straightening at 5 o'clock every day. After it's done, the kids are allowed
to watch some TV while I fix dinner.

Pat Slater
Takoma Park, Maryland

Pacifiers

There are two kinds of infants: those who like pacifiers and those who don't. And there are two kinds of parents: those who use pacifiers and those who wish they could. There are plenty of reasons not to use a pacifier, and many parents have their own reasons for not using this quieting tool. But if you're inclined to try pacifiers, you'll find plenty of useful suggestions in this chapter.

Children need to suck until they are about three years old, so we never made a big deal out of the fact that our two boys used pacifiers until they were three. When our youngest was approaching four, we set a date with him to give up his pacifier, and he literally threw it out the window on that date.

Laurie Palmer
Takoma Park, Maryland

If you decide to use a pacifier for your baby, make the decision (for older babies) that you will only give it to him at night and nap time. Then the baby will only connect the pacifier with sleeping and won't want it all the time. Keep two or three pacifiers in the bed so the baby can always find one and not wake you up by crying for one.

Marty Gregg
Webster Groves, Missouri

I asked our pediatrician to have a heart-to-heart talk with Shannon about her pacifier when she was in her twos. He simply told her that it was time to stop using it—she listened better to him than to me!

Debbie Marklin
Reading, Pennsylvania

It is often difficult to find a pacifier—even when you, or the child, just put it down a second ago. After a calamitous pacifier search at Disney World, we tied an old diaper to the pacifier—and we could always spot it after that.

Sandy Egan
Princeton, New Jersey

When you buy your baby's first pacifier, make sure it's a common one that is in plentiful supply in your area. My son became addicted to a "Binky" pacifier but, for a reason unbeknownst to me, the store I first bought it at stopped carrying it. I couldn't find it anywhere and ended up ordering more pacifiers directly from the manufacturer at great bother and extra expense.

Sandra Fletcher
Silver Spring, Maryland

Have your baby get used to different pacifiers or variations of the same basic kind. Margaret got stuck on hospital-issue pacifiers and we had to go back to the hospital to replenish our supply. With Claire, we have varied her selection enough that she doesn't demand one type.

Jan Hernon
St. Louis, Missouri

A pacifier really helped to calm Nick down, but sometimes when he was fussing and unhappy he would just push the pacifier out with his tongue. When that happened I would gently slide the pacifier back in, and then before he had a chance to either suck on it or push it away, I'd slide it back out again. I'd repeat that action 5 or 10 times. The now-it's-here-now-it's-not motion seemed to make him want to try to hang on to it, and when I finally let him get his mouth around it, he'd suck on it contentedly.

Tina Bachman
Rockville, Maryland

Try different pacifiers until you find one that works. Never give up. Eventually, you may find one that your baby likes enough to quiet him down.

Sally Anga
Seattle, Washington

Parenting Resources

If this book has demonstrated one thing, it is that you are not alone. With every problem you've had, some other parent has been there before. With every peculiar thing your toddler has done, some other baby has also done that same thing. And for every problem you have, there are parents around the country who can give you advice. The following suggestions provide the names of books, organizations, and programs that have helped many parents and may help you, too.

There are two half-hour TV shows carried over most cable services that I've found very helpful, especially in those first few months as a new parent. They are both on the Family Channel. One is called the "American Baby Show." The second is called "Healthy Kids," produced in association with the American Academy of Pediatrics. Check your local cable guide for schedules.

Judith Gordon
Washington, D.C.

Playgrounds are for parents, too. When you're feeling isolated, especially with an infant, head for the playground. You'll usually find some welcome companionship, a sympathetic ear, maybe even a new friend.

Mary Rowley
Strongsville, Ohio

I really enjoy using Vicki Lansky's *Feed Me! I'm Yours.* It offers lots of suggestions for feeding babies, good kid-appealing recipes, and holiday and birthday advice.

Lisa Reutzloff
St. Ann, Missouri

Solve Your Child's Sleep Problem by Richard Ferber is an excellent resource. It helps parents with sleep-related issues for children of all ages, from infants on up. It offers very clear, simple advice.

> *Jan Hernon*
> *St. Louis, Missouri*

La Leche League was an invaluable help to me with my newborn, not just for breast-feeding problems but also for helping me cope with the overwhelming experience of being a new mother without any family in town for support. The monthly La Leche League meetings introduced me to new friends and gave me a lot of reassurance about the way I was dealing with my baby. La Leche League has chapters in all major cities and many smaller towns as well. Call 1-800-LA-LECHE to find the group nearest you.

> *Nora T. Burns*
> *Alexandria, Virginia*

The Perfectly Safe catalog has a number of useful, innovative items that you don't find in other children's product stores or catalogs—such as replacement straps for high chairs, lid locks for toilet seats, and fire-rescue decals for children's bedroom windows. Order it by calling 1-800-837-KIDS or by writing to Perfectly Safe, 7245 Whipple Ave., N.W., North Canton, OH 44720.

> *Elizabeth Kreigh*
> *Bellaire, Texas*

Get *Your Baby and Child—From Birth to Age Five* by Penelope Leach. It's an excellent book with a good, commonsense approach to everyday care and all situations of child rearing.

> *Various parents*

I loved *The Mother's Almanac* by Marguerite Kelly and Elia Parsons. The book was written by two mothers and has a lot of great ideas.

> *Laurie Palmer*
> *Takoma Park, Maryland*

Check with your local school district to see if they offer a Parents as First Teachers program. In this program you meet other parents and your toddler has a chance to start socializing. It's a great way to receive valuable parenting information.

Marty Gregg
Webster Groves, Missouri

With so many great baby and toddler products available by catalog, you may never have to leave your house to get the things your kids need. Many time-saving items are easy to order in many child-oriented specialty catalogs but are hard to find in stores. We highly recommend the following catalogs, which can be ordered by phone:

The Right Start, 1-800-LITTLE-1
One Step Ahead, 1-800-274-8440
Sensational Beginnings, 1-800-444-2147
Phases for Kids, 1-800-874-9887
Hand in Hand, 1-800-872-9745
Just for Kids, 1-800-654-6963
The Great Kids Company, 1-800-533-2166
Lilly's Kids, 1-914-633-6300
Sesame Street—The Catalog, 1-800-367-8995

Bill Adler, Jr., and
Peggy Robin
Washington, D.C.

Photography and Videotaping

Quiz: Could the photography and VCR industries survive without children? Is that a question that even has to be asked? These days, it seems that one of the rites of parenthood is acquiring a video camera. We were reluctant to get one, but when we finally did we discovered that sometimes we enjoyed watching Karen on tape more than in real life. We have no idea why, but Karen likes watching herself on tape, too. Read on for some additional observations and tips.

For better birthday-party videos, a firm directional hand is needed. Know in advance what scenes you're going to film and when they'll take place. Don't just set up the camera and let it roll unless you have the capability and patience to edit it later. A few minutes of each event will be enough to capture the flavor. More than one episode of Pin the Tail on the Donkey and your friends and family will die of boredom!

Jane Donnelly
Meriden, Connecticut

Starting at birth, take a photo of your child once a month (or once every two, three, or four months) in a simple outfit, perhaps a T-shirt and pants, in the same spot and pose each time. Mounting the photos in progression on a wall or in an album will give a wonderful speed-up-motion effect of the child growing before your eyes. We intend to keep our photo growth chart going until our kids have moved away from home.

Angie Nathanson
Sweden, Maine

Bring your camera when you get together with your friends and their kids during the year. Then include photos of *your friends'* kids with your Christmas card to show them how much you enjoyed seeing them. I never knew what to do with the photos I took of other people's kids, but a friend sent me a picture of my daughter at a birthday party and I loved having it!

> *Maggie Keely Foley*
> *Kirkwood, Missouri*

We had some particularly cute shots of our firstborn: Laura eating spaghetti at nine months, Laura holding on to my hands while she walked at 11 months. When our two boys reached those same ages, we took similar shots of them. Now we have a terrific series of three pictures. In our kitchen we have a photo of each of our children with an orange, spaghetti-smeared face. In our living room, we have a wonderful group featuring each of our babies grasping my fingers as he or she learned to walk.

> *Mary Ellen Koenig*
> *Takoma Park, Maryland*

Don't try to be both a camera operator and participant. Let one parent or adult supervise the activity, leaving the other free to concentrate on holding the camera and getting the good shots.

> *Steve Grunwald*
> *Milwaukee, Wisconsin*

We always have a VCR tripod on hand for birthday parties so that when our photographer (my husband) is needed to help maintain some semblance of order, light candles, hold the piñata, or clean up a spill, we can keep the VCR rolling to catch the action.

> *Brigid O'Toole*
> *Pleasant Hill, California*

For indoor shots, to avoid red-eye try using high-speed film in a room with good lighting. This way, no flash is needed.

> *Dave Dryden*
> *Louisville, Kentucky*

Every two years, starting when my kids were newborns, I took pictures of a day in their lives so that grandparents who lived far away would know what their lives were like. Sometimes it would take a week or more to get 15 pictures to include in the picture book. The book always started "Dear Grandmother and Granddaddy" and ended each time with a picture of them asleep in their beds. Sometimes they drew pictures to go in the book or dictated words to me to write under a picture. The kids would sign their names at the end when they were old enough. My kids are in their 20s now, but when we visit their grandparents, we still see the books I sent when my two children were young.

Jo Hoge
Takoma Park, Maryland

Always get two sets of photos, one for you and one for friends and relatives. Put one set in an album immediately, or you lose control quickly.

Various parents

Here's a videotaping tip your family will appreciate: Get action shots instead of waiting and waiting and waiting for the baby to turn over.

Peggy Robin
Washington, D.C.

It's great to have photo postcards of the baby to send to relatives, but it's a lot of trouble to take the negatives to a photo store every few months to have a current set of postcards made up. So here's what I do: I pick a nice three-by-five-inch photo and apply double-sided tape all around the edges on the back, stick it to the lined side of a three-by-five-inch index card, and use the blank side to write the name, address, and a brief note. Then I just stick a postcard stamp in the corner and pop it in the mail.

Fran German
Ft. Lauderdale, Florida

On videotaping: have music playing in the background. A catchy hit song can help you recall the mood of the time when you watch the video years from now. Music also makes toddlers livelier.

Peggy Robin
Washington, D.C.

Don't have the same parent always do the shooting. If Daddy's always the photographer, he's never in the picture! (Besides, if Daddy has a tendency to take head shots only, you want the variety of another photographer.) If one of the parents claims to be hopeless at operating the device, get one of those error-free models that set focus, exposure, flash, and film speed, plus wind and rewind automatically.

Mark Lynch
Los Angeles, California

Many parents like to make their own Christmas cards using a good family photograph. But the pictures are always so stiffly posed, so boring! Mom, Dad, kids, and family dog, all sitting on a sofa, just like all the other family-photo Christmas cards your friends send out each year. This year do something different! How about a picture of you all splashing in a pool on the hottest day in July? What if all of you were wearing Santa Claus hats and beards and red suits (including the dog)? Or Mom and Dad sitting on a sled with the kids trying to pull? Or any other action shot you can set up. Think unusual, think fun—and be sure to shoot lots of pictures, just in case a few don't come out well.

Jessica Moore
Seattle, Washington

For great baby pictures you have to be willing to waste film. Quantity will eventually produce quality. In other words, if you keep snapping away, eventually you'll catch the baby in one or two shots per roll with a huge grin on his face, doing something absolutely adorable.

Jamie Robinson
New York, New York

When videotaping, don't yell out directions when the tape is rolling. Your instructions will dominate the tape. Similarly, tell other adults in the room to be quiet. Just let the baby be the star of the show.

Peggy Robin
Washington, D.C.

Patience is the key—I mean the parent's patience, not the baby's. I wait with my camera loaded and ready until my baby's in the right mood. I stop shooting as soon as she seems tired, bored, cranky, or hungry. Sometimes I don't try again until hours later or even the next day.

May Clarke
New York, New York

Some parents shoot all their baby pictures from their adult level looking down at the baby, and usually getting the top of their baby's head. Other parents sit the baby on a couch or in a high chair and shoot up, usually giving you a great look inside the baby's nostrils. The best pictures, though, are usually taken at baby's-eye level.

Joyce Sommers
Washington, D.C.

A little preparation can really contribute to great pictures. For studio-like portrait shots I clear the background of all clutter, cover the rug with a soft, blue blanket, and sit a life-size baby doll in the middle. Then I can practice camera angles and sharpen the focus on a stand-in that doesn't fuss at all over how long I'm taking. When I've got the camera ready, I bring in Jon and substitute him for the baby doll. My husband stands behind me holding a furry rabbit puppet, talking to Jon in his Mr. Bunny voice so Jon will look toward the camera and smile. When Jon gets bored with Mr. Bunny, I hand him a ball and take his picture as he holds it. When he's done with that, I give him a colorful rattle. The best picture I have of him, though, is the one I took after I handed him a picture book. There he is, six months old, apparently engrossed in his book. Everyone tells me that picture is professional quality.

Chris Anderson
San Francisco,
California

Many times I've captured my toddler with a terrific expression on his face, but the picture is not a great one because it's not well framed—he's too far to one side, or there's someone else in the picture who didn't come out well, or any number of other reasons. But I've discovered the wonders of enlargement and cropping. At some photo stores you can slide your negative into a viewer that shows you what your picture will look like blown up to five-by-seven or eight-by-ten and then you can adjust the viewing area to crop out whatever side of the picture you don't like. Then you press a button, and a few moments later you have a custom enlarged print.

Carol O'Neill
Rockville, Maryland

Playpens and Walkers

We were talking with a friend of ours, Marta, who is also a parent, about the question of when our children should graduate from a crib to a junior bed. "It's a matter of safety," we said to Marta. Marta shot back, "Not entirely—once Karen's in a bed, she'll be able to get out and walk around and into your bedroom whenever she wants." Hmm. Playpens, and walkers, like cribs, are prisons of sorts. But used affectionately, your child can have more fun in them than practically anywhere else, as you'll see in this chapter.

An inflatable wading pool can make a terrific playpen for a small baby. Inexpensive, sized right, and safe, a pool-as-playpen has one other advantage: Your rug or floor won't get drooled on.

Bill Davis
Woodstock, New York

Instead of a playpen, which Sara would find small and confining, we created a totally baby-safe playroom for her to play in. All outlets are covered, the floor is thickly carpeted, the phone is mounted high on the wall, there are no plants or lamps to knock over, and no movable objects anywhere in reach except for toys and other things that are okay for her to touch. This playroom is just off the kitchen; we put a barrier between the two rooms so I can cook or clean up and still see and hear Sara and be just a few steps away if she needs me.

Gloria Buttenweiser
Andover, Massachusetts

When you're out in the yard in hot weather, put your toddler in a playpen with a hose tied to the rail. Let a small trickle of running water come out of the hose for your child to play in.

Frances Noonan
Kirkwood, Missouri

If you've got a basement door, a child in a walker, and an older child, you've got the ingredients for disaster. Invest in a small sliding lock that is installed near the top of the door so that only adults can unlock it and use it!

Mary Rowley
Strongsville, Ohio

If you're going to use a playpen—and I did for each of my four children—use it from the beginning. Put them in as early as three months so they are comfortable with being in it. If you only put them in when they start to move around, they will view it as a prison.

Jill Hansen
Dubuque, Iowa

We always took our playpen to the beach and set it up on a beach blanket—upside down! This provided the much-needed shade for the baby when he or she was sleeping.

Snowden Kirby-Smith
Washington, D.C.

Reading

From one month to about one year, babies consider books to be a major food group. After that, however, they are endlessly amused and entertained by the words and pictures. Your child will probably want to hear the same book read over and over again until you all know it by heart. In this chapter parents share their thoughts and views on the wonderful world of reading.

It's never too early to begin lifelong habits. We started reading to our children when they were each about two months old, and they loved it. We would lie on the floor and hold a brightly colored book above their heads, turning the pages and reading aloud. Babies react to it like a mobile, eagerly watching the changing shapes, kicking their heels, and squealing.

Bob Koenig
Takoma Park, Maryland

When our preschoolers were learning the alphabet, we would often take "letter walks." We would pick one letter and look for that letter while we walked to the store, park, or wherever. We would find the day's letter on signs, trucks, even manhole covers.

Elizabeth Kreigh
Bellaire, Texas

We weren't reading on a regular basis (except at bedtime) until we started making Friday our library day. Establishing a weekly routine has been really good for us. We keep the library books in a box near the couch. After the girls have heard a story several times, I encourage them to "read" to their dolls.

Margaret Edelman
Garden City, New York

The Randolph J. Caldecott Medal has been awarded annually since 1938 to the illustrator of the most distinguished picture book for children published in the United States during the previous year. It's kind of nice to break up the monotony of kiddie junk books with some quality books, whether you get them from the library or buy them. When the kids get older, they might be interested in the winners of the John Newbery Medal. Here are a few of the Caldecott winners from recent years:

> *Tuesday* by David Wiesner (1992)
> *Black and White* by David Macaulay (1991)
> *Lon Po Po: A Red Riding Hood Story from China*,
>   translated by Ed Young (1990)
> *Song and Dance Man* by Karen Ackerman (1989)
> *Owl Moon* by Jane Yolen (1988)
> *Hey, Al* by Arthur Yorinks (1987)
> *The Polar Express* by Chris Van Allsburg (1986)
> *St. George and the Dragon*,
>   adapted by Margaret Hodges (1985)
> *Arrow to the Sun* by George McDermott (1975)
> *Sam, Bangs & Moonshine* by Evaline Ness (1967)
> *Where the Wild Things Are* by Maurice Sendak (1964)

Mary Ellen Koenig
Takoma Park, Maryland

Paul learned to say his ABC's by stacking blocks. As we stacked the blocks higher and higher, I sang the alphabet song; he learned it quickly.

Kathy Ladd
St. Louis, Missouri

Most large cities now have children's bookstores with wonderful selections and knowledgeable salespeople. But for those who don't have access to these resources, get a catalog from the Chinaberry Book Service. It's like having a good children's bookstore arrive in your mailbox. The catalog has a wonderful selection and gives a detailed description of each book. To get on their mailing list, call 1-800-776-2242 or write to Chinaberry Book Service, 2830 Via Orange Way, Ste. B, Spring Valley, CA 92078.

Betsy Siebert
Lenexa, Kansas

I labeled many things in Jenny's room, such as "bed," "door," and "window." Those words were the first words she learned to read.

Sue Poness
Takoma Park, Maryland

My husband makes a monthly chart on the computer highlighting special dates for the girls. It also includes a simple word for the day—usually just a three- or four-letter word. The calendar is posted on the refrigerator, and every morning the girls move one circular magnet to the day of the week and one magnet to the actual date. We all look at the word of the day at that time, too.

Patty Bohn
Webster Groves, Missouri

Keep a roll of tape handy whenever you read pop-up books to your toddler. Kids do love them, but they also have a tendency to rip out some of the best pop-up characters in these books. Then they get upset because the book is "broken." But you can usually make it look as good as new with a few sutures of cosmetic tape surgery.

"Dr." Ellen Porter
Larchmont, New York

The Dr. Seuss books are great to read to toddlers because of all the wonderful rhymes, but the books are rather long for bedtime material. So I just read the first rhyme or two on each page. With books like *One Fish Two Fish Red Fish Blue Fish* that have no storyline, it doesn't matter if you leave things out. But to get away with this form of abridgment, you've got to start doing it the first time you read the book. Otherwise, they'll get used to hearing the whole thing and will recognize when you've skipped over something.

Betsy Messenger
Providence, Rhode Island

When I read a picture book to my 17-month-old, I hardly ever bother with the actual text that accompanies each picture. The writing is usually boring and dumb. I like to get my child involved in the book by asking her to point to certain things on the page. I say, "Where's the elephant?" and even though she can't say elephant yet, she can pick it out correctly all the time. I say, "Show me the blue balloon" and "Which is the red balloon?" and she learns colors, even if the book isn't about colors at all. When I know that she can say a word for something in the book, I ask her, "What's that?" and then she says "cat" or "moo-cow" or whatever it is. She seems to enjoy this a lot more than just sitting and having me read.

Melanie Worth
Walnut Creek, California

Keep your library books in one special place at all times—separate from your other books. And make sure that everyone in the family understands that that's where the books belong when they are not being read. That way you aren't searching under beds and on crowded bookshelves when the books are due.

Anne Morrison
Lansing, Michigan

Safety

There's no doubt that safety is paramount in parents' minds. Fortunately, many of the potential dangers that a baby can face have been eliminated by medicine and careful manufacturing of baby products. The remainder of these potential dangers can be addressed by taking an infant first-aid and CPR class and by common sense. Still, every baby is going to get a bump and a scrape now and then. The good news is that the pain and crying pass quickly. Read on for tips on how to keep your child safe.

If your preschooler likes to play dress-up, make sure she (or he) only wears pop-bead necklaces. Other necklaces can get caught on slides, staircases, or just by falling down, and can result in strangulation.

Susan Carlson
Alexandria, Virginia

We have two banisters on our stairs, a higher one for the adults and a lower one for the children. Having a child-size banister helps teach the little ones to get safely up the stairs.

Emily van Loon
Takoma Park, Maryland

In our household we have a number of rules that were established when the kids were very little. These rules are nonnegotiable, meaning no discussion will be tolerated. The rules include:
• Sticks are not toys.
• Seat belts and car seats are used at all times.
• Children must always wear life jackets at the lake.
• Children may not set foot in the street without holding an adult's hand.

Anne O'Brien
Sandusky, Ohio

We have a special chair in the living room to sit in when someone needs comforting from a fall, a scratch, a bump, whatever. We don't call it the magic chair or anything, but always going to the same place seems to have a quieting effect.

Terry Clifford
Takoma Park, Maryland

It is definitely worth the extra expense to have a gate at the top of the stairs as well as at the bottom of the stairs. That way you are not constantly running up and down to position the gate—you always have one where you need it.

Jo Mannies
Webster Groves, Missouri

To bring home the facts of how a car can hurt a person, I had my young children help me fill a bag with simple items: a ball of aluminum foil, a plastic fork, and other things. We placed the bag in the driveway and I drove over it with the car. The results helped me to stress the importance of using extreme caution near streets and parking lots.

Veronica Campbell
Chesterfield, Missouri

Teach your children very early that they should always ask a dog's owner for permission to pet a dog before doing so.

Trish Cody
Austin, Texas

Before your baby starts walking—and certainly before he starts running—be sure that you have something under area rugs and doormats to keep them from sliding.

Maureen Alexander
Chicago, Illinois

Tie little jingle bells to your children's shoelaces when they are very little. Children love to hear the sound when they walk and adults always know where the baby is from the sound. When you don't hear the sound, you know it's time to find out what they are up to. Make sure your child can't get to the bells by enclosing them in some of the plastic shoelace holders made to protect the bells from little hands.

Cathy Shirski
Boston, Massachusetts

It's helpful to occasionally invoke the names of other authority figures such as your pediatrician, dentist, or the child's teacher. It puts you on the side of the child when you say "Dr. So-and-So says it's important that we drink our milk" or "Dr. Such-and-Such says we have to brush our teeth every night."

Marianne Alweiss
New York, New York

Never carry your baby downstairs while you are wearing just socks.

Harp Matthews
Dallas, Texas

Caution with hotel cribs. One hotel we stayed at tried to make their cribs more comfortable (or so they thought) by putting a double mattress in the crib. We awoke in the middle of the night to hear Karen screaming because she had gotten caught between the mattress and crib bars—the double mattress had given her room to slide down. Other hotels we've stayed at have offered tiny pillows with their cribs—a definite suffocation risk for infants.

Bill Adler, Jr.
Washington, D.C.

Parents who worry when leaving a baby under a year old with a sitter may find it worthwhile to get a cellular phone or beeper so the sitter can call them in case of emergency. Beepers are relatively inexpensive and offer great peace of mind.

Mark Lovitt
Englewood, New Jersey

Put your stair barrier two or three steps from the bottom of carpeted stairs so your baby can practice going up and down a few steps. We did this with Justin and he loved being able to climb a couple of steps. The area at the base of our stairs wasn't carpeted, so I put a big quilt down to cushion his fall.

Hope Langley
Richmond, Virginia

We have all our kitchen cabinets and drawers safety-latched except one cabinet at floor level. We call this our toddler-exploring cabinet. She opens the door and finds old plastic coasters, Tupperware bowls, dish towels, animal-shaped potholders, plastic trays, and all kinds of interesting things that she can pull out with no harm done either to the objects or to her.

Peggy Robin
Washington, D.C.

The Juvenile Products Manufacturers Association (JPMA) has a free brochure called *Be Sure It's Safe for Your Baby.* Write JPMA, 2 Greentree Ctr., Ste. 225, Box 955, Marlton, NJ 08053.

Various parents

Make a wallet-size emergency reference card to carry in your stroller bag, diaper bag, and car and to give out to babysitters. Type or write clearly on a piece of paper these important phone numbers: your office, spouse's office, pediatrician's office, pediatrician's answering service (if it's a different number), ambulance or hospital, your own doctor's office, neighbor's home, and any other numbers or information that might be of particular use to you in an emergency (child's blood type, for example, or a grandparent's phone number). Take the paper to a photocopy shop and have it reduced to make the information small enough to fit into a credit card–size space. Be sure to make lots of copies. Then cut some index cards down to credit-card size. Center the phone reference list over the card, glue it down, and trim away the excess paper. Buy some adhesive laminating plastic at an office supply store and cover the card with it so that it won't crumple or rip.

Vanessa Cole
Rockville, Maryland

Here's a six-step plan for dealing with the medicine cabinet:

1. Go through the cabinet and throw out all medicines and products that have passed their expiration dates. If there's no expiration date, but you can't remember when you bought the product, it's too old. Throw it out.
2. Throw out any medicines that don't have childproof caps.
3. Remove any items that belong elsewhere, such as household cleaners. When you need syrup of ipecac in the middle of the night, you shouldn't have to shove aside bottles of drain opener and mildew spray to find the right product.
4. Make sure you have the following items on hand:
   • isopropyl alcohol (for sterilizing)
   • cotton balls/cotton swabs
   • acetaminophen (for infant or child, depending on your kids' ages)
   • syrup of ipecac (to induce vomiting in some instances of poisoning, according to directions of your nearest poison control center)
   • bacitracin (or any other form of antibiotic ointment)
   • medicine spoon, dropper, or syringe (your doctor will tell you what is the best method for getting your child to take liquid by mouth)
   • tweezers
   • children's cough medicine
   • hydrocortisone cream (to treat rashes and skin irritations as your doctor directs)
   • plastic bandages for small cuts
   • sterile gauze pads and paper tape for larger cuts
   • rectal thermometer
   • petroleum jelly
   • nasal aspirator (to remove mucus from nasal passages of an infant with a head cold)
5. Separate items for your own use from your child's. Use two different medicine cabinets if possible. If you don't have two, put adult items on a separate high shelf. You will be far less likely to mistakenly give your toddler a spoonful of adult cough medicine once you have taken this step.
6. Put a childproof cabinet latch or lock on the medicine-cabinet door.

Peter A. Wright
Cambridge,
Massachusetts

A registered nurse told me about a plastic tube you can buy to test a baby's toys to see whether they're too small and might present a choking hazard. But just as good as the purchased tester-tube, she said, is the empty cardboard toilet-paper cylinder. If a toy or any loose part of a toy will fit inside that cylinder, then it's too small to be given safely to a baby.

Jody Johnson
Palo Alto, California

I wanted to make sure that my tap water was safe, that the interior and exterior wall paint was lead-free, and that the glaze on my imported ceramic dinnerware was completely nontoxic. First I called my local health department and found out there was a free lead-testing program for homes with small children. To test the paint and the dinnerware I bought my own lead-testing kit at a well-stocked hardware store. The kit was under $20, had easy-to-follow directions, and gave results in just a few minutes. If you don't find the kit in a store you can order one from the Safety Zone catalog—call 1-800-999-3030.

Anne Holbrooks
Knoxville, Tennessee

To prevent your toddler from having a door accidentally close on her little fingers while she's examining the door hinge, you can buy a simple, inexpensive device that hooks over the hinge and prevents anyone from closing the door accidentally. This was especially helpful for us because our older child, Mark, didn't pay attention to where Jackie's hands were when he went to close a door.

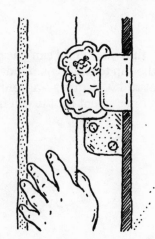

Grace Adler
Atlanta, Georgia

A rubber-wedged door stop can be stuck in a door hinge to prevent the door from accidentally closing on a toddler's fingers.

Kathy Fink
Los Angeles, California

The Red Cross puts out posters that show step by step how to do rescue breathing and CPR and the Heimlich maneuver on an infant or child. Hang these on the inside of the door to each bathroom, and make sure that all caregivers know they're there. The poster is available in Spanish, too.

Dana Marquez
Charlestown,
West Virginia

I like to look for bargains on baby equipment at yard sales, but I'm concerned about the safety of not-so-new high chairs, strollers, doorway jumpers, and so forth. So I apply this standard: If the product bears a "Certified" tag or sticker from the JPMA (Juvenile Products Manufacturers Association) and the sticker is not so torn or faded as to be unreadable, then I know that the product is not too old (at least it doesn't predate the JPMA's 15-year-old certification program) and must have been reasonably well maintained for the sticker to still be intact.

Margo Dibold
Takoma Park, Maryland

To be sure that your child can't accidentally scald himself when he turns on the tap to wash his hands, turn down your hot water heater thermostat to 120 degrees Fahrenheit. That's hot enough for an adult shower, but not so hot that it will injure a child.

Lisa K. Hoyer
Morgantown,
West Virginia

I have this reminder list by the side of my stove—not just for my sitter but for myself as well:

Did you remember...
to turn pot handles toward the wall?
to keep mugs of hot liquid away from the edge of the table?
to fasten the safety strap when baby is in the high chair?

Bobbi Kahn
Ypsilanti, Michigan

Whenever I go outside with my toddler I always take a cordless phone with me. That way I'm not tempted to run inside "just for a minute" to find out who it is when I hear the phone ring.

Stephanie Friebus
Albuquerque,
New Mexico

We wanted our little girl to learn to say her full name, address, and phone number as soon as she possibly could, so if she ever got lost she could tell someone who she was. But at two and a half she just couldn't speak clearly enough to say all that information in a way someone else could understand. However, we noticed that she was able to remember and sing all the words to a song quite well. So I arranged all the information we wanted her to know to the tune of "Twinkle, Twinkle, Little Star." She learned to sing:

"Alice Turner is my name
And I live on Bradley Lane
555-9123
That is how you can call me
Alice Turner is my name
And I live on Bradley Lane."

Of course, other parents will have to rewrite the song to suit their children, and maybe find a different tune, too; we have friends who worked their two girls' names and phone number into the theme song from the "Patty Duke Show."

Marty Turner
Chevy Chase, Maryland

I like to take our kids for walks in the woods, but I don't want them exposed to Lyme disease from ticks, so we take some precautions. I dress our infant in light, long-sleeve playsuits with attached feet, and I put our four-year-old in long pants that tuck into boots (when it's too hot for boots, she wears thick socks that I can roll up over the cuffs of her lightweight pants). And since we know that Lyme disease–carrying ticks prefer animal fur, we leave our poodle at home.

Lon Garwood
Monticello, New York

Since so many parents use disposable diapers these days, some diaper services have branched out into other areas of baby care. Our diaper service also does babyproofing of houses. They sent a baby-safety expert out to our house to cap all our outlets and install cabinet latches and stairway gates. They alerted us to all the safety hazards in our house. It's more expensive than a do-it-yourself babyproofing, of course, but professional babyproofers don't miss anything, and they're a lot better at installation than an unhandy couple like us.

Lori Bartlett
Bethesda, Maryland

I needed 20 or so outlet covers, 12 cabinet latches, and 8 drawer latches, plus corner guards and switch covers and a great many other products to babyproof the house. But when I went shopping and saw the variety of products available, I didn't know which products to buy. So I bought just one of each type of latch, one of each type of corner guard, and one of each type of electric-cord reel, and tried them at home to find out which was easiest to install and most convenient to use. Once I knew the type of drawer latches I wanted, I bought another seven. Though I had to make two trips to the store, that was still a lot easier than installing all the drawer latches at once, finding out that they were difficult to use, unscrewing them, and going back to the store to get another style.

Fred Hudgenson
Fairfax, Virginia

Never, ever have balloons at a party for young children. I had heard of a child who got his hands on an uninflated balloon, put it in his mouth, choked, and died. The Heimlich maneuver was not successful in bringing the rubbery mass back up. Even inflated balloons are dangerous because they can easily pop, and before you know it, a child could be sucking on the remnants.

Jennifer Southerland
Atlanta, Georgia

Be careful not to say "Be careful" too much.

Kathleen Winters
Tempe, Arizona

Shopping

Babies and toddlers love to go shopping. They like being driven around in the shopping cart, and they especially like grabbing things off the shelves as your attention wanders to something else.

If your baby is old enough to sit up with some support, but you don't want to lug a baby seat into the grocery store, simply go to the paper-towel aisle first. Get two big rolls of towels and put one on each side of the baby for support. You can either put the towels back when you are finished shopping or buy them! You *always* need paper towels.

Aloysia Hamalainen
Silver Spring, Maryland

Karen is old enough to sit on the seat of a supermarket cart, but she's still a little wobbly when she's in it. I find that my Snugli front carrier can be used to provide her with some padding and also function as a seat belt for extra security. The padded shoulder straps go behind and in front of her, and the snap-in ends attach to the shopping cart to hold her securely in place.

Peggy Robin
Washington, D.C.

Whenever I have Jennifer with me at the supermarket, I pick up a couple of brochures for magazines that are displayed near the checkout lines. There are always brochures for pet and wildlife magazines, and these usually occupy Jennifer for the duration of the shopping expedition.

Carrie Gerard
Flagstaff, Arizona

Carry your child in a side carrier or front carrier rather than in a backpack or in the shopping cart seat. This way you don't have to worry about your child grabbing things off the shelves as you walk down the aisles.

Kevin Mitchell
Washington, D.C.

Now I choose my malls carefully. Unless there's a place to nurse and change Danielle, I don't shop there.

Susan Connor
Wilmington, Delaware

To prevent your child from grabbing items off the supermarket shelves while she sits in the shopping cart, make sure she's got plenty of her own snacks and toys to occupy her hands and mouth. Cookies or crackers are easiest to take along in a zip-lock baggie. Also, be sure your child is well fed before you go; she'll be less intent on grabbing boxes with pictures of food on them.

Abby Massie
Seattle, Washington

When we're running errands, I use the time that I'm cruising for a parking space to verbally rehearse with the girls what we will do when we're in the store. Also, I mention their restrictions ("Stay by Mommy," "Hold the cart," "No running," "Don't ask Mommy to buy anything today"). Whenever I talk through the shopping trip ahead of time, the whole expedition goes more smoothly.

Margaret Edelman
Garden City, New York

It's a mistake to take a baby or toddler with you if you're shopping for your own clothes or making a major purchase. You'll end up with a screaming child and a purchase you didn't intend to make—or, alternatively, nothing at all. Instead of taking the child with you, find a friend who would also enjoy some time in a store by herself, and trade child-care responsibilities.

Martha Shirk
Webster Groves, Missouri

Ever since I had the baby I've hardly been in a grocery store. I do nearly all my shopping through a grocery home-delivery service. I just call up the service and read off my list. If I'm at work, I don't even have to make a call; I can fax in my order. The service I use has a fixed delivery charge, but the prices of the items are slightly cheaper than in the stores. On a big order I actually spend less. I can arrange for a very early morning delivery or an evening delivery when I'm home from work. I get all my bulk items that way: diapers, wipes, baby food and formula, paper towels, big bottles of laundry detergent, dog food, you name it. The service I use is called Tele-grocery. Friends in other big cities have told me that similar services are available there, too.

Martha Davis
Crystal City, Virginia

I think the key to grocery shopping with your child is to keep him busy: Give him things to hold, have him find things for you or help pick out the fruit, give an older child a list with two or three items and read it together before sending him to find the items in the aisle you are in, or ask him to rearrange the bottom of the shopping cart. Make sure your child knows that you are only buying things on the list, so that when the candy issue comes up, you can say, "It's not on the list."

Liz Malone
Silver Spring, Maryland

Go food shopping at lunchtime and feed your toddler as you shop. Make the first stop at the bakery and get a roll, then give him a piece of cheese or a slice of turkey. By the time you're at the checkout line, he'll be ready for dessert (which he can have if he has behaved).

Sandy Egan
Princeton, New Jersey

When grocery shopping, ask the bagger to put all the frozen foods and perishables in a separate bag or two. When you get home, you only have to get out a few bags—and the baby—from the car. Leave the rest until you've got the baby comfortable.

Kitty Berra
St. Louis, Missouri

I got a stroller big enough to hold my two kids. I brought it whenever I went shopping at a mall or large store and let them sit in it until they were five and six years old. I didn't worry about what the stroller looked like—my kids enjoyed being pushed around, and I liked having them in one place.

Jo Mannies
Webster Groves, Missouri

Siblings

If one baby is so wonderful, two must be even better, right? Just ask the firstborn child. I (Peggy) have a brother, Richard, who's three years older. When I was born, my parents got a live-in nanny to help take care of me for the first few weeks. Soon it was time for the nanny to leave. When she stepped out the door of the house, Richard ran after her, yelling, "Wait, you forgot your baby!" In this section you'll find other humorous stories—and tips—about dealing with siblings.

When we were expecting our second child, we repeatedly made the point that our whole family was having a baby, not just Mommy. Even though Elinor was only three, we made sure we included her when we picked a name for the new baby.

Carol Mermey
San Francisco,
California

It really bothered Maggie when I nursed Matthew, so I encouraged her to "nurse" one of her dolls at the same time.

Jo Mannies
Webster Groves, Missouri

To help a first child with the arrival of a new baby, take two wrapped presents for the older child when you leave for the hospital. When the sibling comes to meet his new brother or sister, the older child can receive a gift from Mom and the new baby. Also, it's a good idea to keep some small wrapped presents at home for the older child when people come by with gifts for the new baby. It gives the older child some needed attention.

Marty Gregg
Webster Groves, Missouri

It breaks your heart to introduce your second baby to your first baby, or your third baby to your second. You can try as hard as you want to prepare the older child, but there's little you can do to prepare yourself. This is not a tip, just a gentle warning.

Mary Ellen Koenig
Takoma Park, Maryland

This is an age-old solution to an age-old problem: When you want to divide something between two children, one child gets to divide or cut the item in half, and the other gets first choice of which piece to take. It works.

Margie Frievogel
Bethesda, Maryland

When Rosie and Lily are having an argument over a particular toy, I give them the kitchen timer and let *them* decide on a fair time limit for each one to play with the toy. This teaches them to settle their own arguments.

Margaret Edelman
Garden City, New York

When two of my children begin to squabble and pick on each other, I send them *together* to a room and tell them that if they can be nice to each other for 10 minutes, then they can come out. If the squabbling continues, the time is extended. What inevitably happens is that after they resolve their problems, they begin playing together again, and after the prescribed 10 minutes, they don't want to come out!

Linda Wilhelm
Washington, D.C.

We took Kevin out of his crib when I was only three months pregnant with our second child because we didn't want him to think that the baby "took" his crib. By the time Kimberly arrived, he was happily adjusted to his new bed.

Rose Krasnow
Rockville, Maryland

Sitters

Once you become a parent, you begin to understand those friends of yours who always used to say, "Sorry, we can't go. We can't get a sitter." But why does it always seem that there's never a sitter around when you need one? Here are some tips on finding and working with babysitters.

When we need a sitter we call the nursing school at the university nearby. We know those sitters are trained to handle all the common first-aid problems and can distinguish between an emergency and a situation that can wait. The ones who take babysitting jobs are often interested in pediatric nursing, and they love children.

Diana Kerr
Falls Church, Virginia

Many Red Cross chapters offer an inexpensive training class for babysitters. We were happy to pay for our sitter to take it, and she was pleased with it too, since it allowed her to charge other parents a slightly higher rate for her certifiable skills.

Alan Wright
Boston, Massachusetts

As your kids get into the toddler stage, look around your neighborhood for a youngster who's interested in being a mother's helper. Ten- or eleven-year-olds are usually too young to babysit, but they are excellent at playing with toddlers and young children while you're home. As your mother's helper gets a little older, he or she will be better prepared to babysit, and you will feel more comfortable knowing that she or he is familiar with your kids, rules, and routines.

Arlene Gottlieb
Silver Spring, Maryland

The first day a new sitter comes, don't vanish right after she arrives. Your kids will accept the new person better if you are with them for a while. Leave when it looks like the kids are having fun or are so caught up in some activity that they'll hardly notice you're gone.

Linda Day Jenkins
Toronto, Canada

We often have a hard time leaving Steve with the sitter when we go out for dinner. Once he's playing with the sitter, Steve is fine. But when we pop in to say goodbye and give the sitter the name of the restaurant and Steve's feeding instructions, he gets an attack of Mommy- and Daddy-itis. So I came up with a simple solution. I just write all the information on a piece of paper and slide it under the door to the room in which the sitter is playing with Steve. That way we not only provide the sitter with all the information she needs, but we also inform her that we're about to leave.

Linda Tulley
Chicago, Illinois

When hiring a sitter I always ask for the names and numbers of two current babysitting clients as references. Some of the questions I ask of these clients are: How old were the children when Jennifer sat for them? Did she follow your instructions well? Did your kids seem to like her? Was she neat? Dependable? Could you trust her judgment, not just in an emergency but in other ways, such as handling your phone messages or knowing when not to answer the doorbell? If you had to make just one criticism of her, what would it be?

I've learned from past experience that if the parent seems uncertain or hesitant in talking about the sitter, it's probably because the parent wasn't totally pleased with the sitter's work but didn't want to ruin her chances of getting another job. When the sitter has been good, the comments are usually glowing, since parents are appreciative of those who are good with their kids. The sitters I've hired who have had less than glowing references always turned out to be unsatisfactory in some way. One left the house a mess, another tied up my phone line for most of the evening, and one even left her leaking pen lying on the table within reach of my baby's grabby fingers and mouth (I fired her on the spot).

Jean Suzuki
Culver City, California

We have a deal with another couple who has a baby a few months older than ours. When we want to go out, they come over and spend the evening at our house, watching our child and their own child while we're gone. We then owe them an evening doing the same at their house. No money changes hands. I've also heard of community associations, clubs, or co-ops that have set up a system to pair up couples willing to sit on certain nights. You register with an office, giving the ages of your kids, your address, and the nights you are available, and the office staff finds you a couple who will stay with your kids when you want to go out. Later they call you to sit for someone else's kids when it's your turn. This system isn't hard to set up if you live in a neighborhood or belong to an organization made up largely of families like your own. You could even advertise on a public bulletin board to find other families nearby who might work with you to set up a regular babysitting exchange.

Allison Orr
Sarasota, Florida

I made up a form to give to all my sitters so that I don't have to spend a lot of time filling them in when they arrive. This way I don't have to worry that they'll forget that bedtime for Lisa is eight-thirty and bedtime for Paul is nine. You can photocopy this form and use it, or custom design your own. Don't forget to fill in the "Important Numbers" section before you make copies.

Margaret Disraeli
Washington, D.C.

Date ....

To ....

Where we'll be ....

Phone number ....

Expected time of return ....

We will call if we will be more than...minutes late

Bedtime is..

Notes about meals or snacks ....

....

....

....

....

....

Notes about bath..

....

....

....

....

....

Other instructions ....
....
....
....
....
....
....
....

Important numbers

Fire department ....ambulance.............................
Pediatrician ....
Other doctors..
Neighbors ....
....
....
Relatives..
....
....

Sleeping

When it comes to sleeping, basically the good old days are gone forever after you become a parent. If you happened to enjoy sleeping in on Sundays until 10 A.M., or 9 A.M., or even 8 A.M., forget it! You'll learn to adapt to your baby or toddler's sleeping habits, but from now on, the little one will be in charge. Still, like most parents, you'll try and try to get your baby to sleep at a particular hour (in time for you to watch "L.A. Law," for example) and get him to stay asleep until a reasonable time (after the morning paper arrives or certainly until "Sesame Street" is on). Good luck! Read on for some advice on how to get children to sleep, from parents who've been there.

Some babies are uncomfortable on a hard crib mattress. For sounder, longer sleeping, try a soft layer of cushioning material under the crib sheet, or buy a lambskin to put on top of the crib sheet.

Carry Nagel
Kingston, New York

When our three-year-old wouldn't go to sleep because he was afraid of monsters, I used "monster spray"—a can of air freshener with a homemade label stating that it repelled monsters.

Suzanne Fleming
Takoma Park, Maryland

When my child complains that he can't go to sleep, I always tell him that he doesn't have to go to sleep—he just has to pretend that he is going to sleep.

Hallie Childs
Washington, D.C.

For getting newborns to sleep, turn the lights down and either sit in a rocker or pace the room with the baby cuddled in your arms. *Gently* massage the baby's forehead with your thumb. Humming or playing soft music is also helpful. Keeping a monotonous rhythm is the key.

Karen Kromm Murphy
Manchester, Missouri

The doctor said my baby no longer needed a night feeding. But Aaron still woke up at least once in the middle of the night and cried and cried until he was fed. We finally devised a plan to get out of this pattern so we could all get a good night's sleep.

I'd tank Aaron up with a long feeding before I put him to bed for the night. Then when he woke up crying at 3 or 4 A.M. I'd go in quietly, not turning on the light, and just rub his back and talk soothingly to him for 10 minutes or until he stopped crying, whichever came first. If he was still crying after 10 minutes, I'd go back to bed, and my husband would go in and rub his back for another 10 minutes or until he stopped crying. If he was still crying hysterically after 20 minutes straight, then I'd come back in and give him a *very* short feeding in his room with the lights dim, and put him right back in his crib. After a few nights of this routine his night-crying jags became shorter and shorter. By the end of the week, he finally had his first night of uninterrupted sleep.

Jenna Davids
Arlington, Virginia

Night terrors can be very frightening—for the parents. You can't wake a child who is in the middle of a night terror, and you shouldn't really try. When Mark was four, he started waking every night, crying loudly and shaking. We would go to him, talk quietly, lead him to the bathroom so he could urinate, and then lead him back to bed. The slow, gentle walk to and from the bathroom seemed to help him settle down when the episode was over. Of course, he never had any memory of the night terrors or of getting up.

Bob Koenig
Takoma Park, Maryland

Let them sleep with their lights on if they want. So what's the big deal?

Various parents

When Jennifer was about three years old, she was waking up with nightmares that left her too scared to go back to sleep. One night I sat down with the doll she always slept with and had a solemn heart-to-heart talk with the doll in front of Jennifer. I told the doll that it was *her* responsibility to make sure that Jennifer didn't have bad dreams. Because she was only three, Jennifer accepted this solution and wasn't afraid to go to sleep.

Diana Cohn
San Francisco,
California

My baby gets scared if he wakes up in the middle of the night and it's dark in his room, but I don't like to leave a light on all night because that would keep *us* awake. So we got a voice-activated night-light. I found it in an electrical supply catalog, but I've since heard that you can buy them in hardware stores. Now when the baby wakes up and cries, the light goes on automatically. It stays on for 10 minutes (you can set it for variable times), and by then he's usually back asleep.

Charles Springer
Charlotte,
North Carolina

When our young children wake up with nightmares, we usually talk them through their fear and tell them that if they describe their dreams out loud, the nightmares will never happen again quite the same way. After we hear what the dreams are about, we help them find solutions. For instance, we say, "If the tiger is chasing you, you can turn around and tell him to stop." The final solution (when all else fails) is, "You can tell yourself to just wake up." The talking is reassuring.

Terry Clifford
Takoma Park, Maryland

My son doesn't mind going to bed if I let him turn out the light himself. He likes to know exactly when it will become dark.

George Sunderland
New Orleans, Louisiana

Move your baby from bed to crib to playpen so that he gets used to sleeping in different places. That way you can comfortably take him to a friend's or Grandma's house and he will be able to sleep.

Betsy Siebert
Lenexa, Kansas

Develop a bedtime routine when your kids are *very* young and stick to it without fail. We always have a small snack before bed, get on p.j.'s, brush teeth, and read a book in Mommy and Daddy's bed before dispersing the kids to their own beds. We rarely alter the routine, and we've never had trouble motivating our three children when we start the process by announcing it's time for a snack.

Elizabeth Kreigh
Bellaire, Texas

When Lily was about 18 months old, she would get so upset when we put her in her crib to sleep—she seemed to regard it as a prison. We dismantled the crib and put her crib mattress on the floor, and that made her so much happier. We didn't have any problem with her getting out of bed, and if she rolled off the mattress, we would simply scoop her up and put her back on.

Margaret Edelman
Garden City, New York

We've played classical music at bedtime ever since the children were infants. It's very soothing. Our older children still love it. And best of all, they have been exposed to wonderful music.

Jeanne LaBella
Alexandria, Virginia

There are some wonderful lullaby tapes that are soothing at bedtime. We love one called "Lullaby Magic," which we bought through Discovery Toys; it has instrumental music on one side and the same songs with words on the other. I have since seen it available in stores.

Mary Pat Hennicke
St. Louis, Missouri

We've found that bedtime is less of a struggle when our 20-month-old is very tired. So we set aside some time after dinner to play some very active games with her. We chase her, play tickling games, bounce her around, and generally try to use up all her excess energy. Then we wind down with a bath, put her in pajamas, brush her teeth, and by the time we've done all that, she's usually ready and willing to lie down and go to sleep.

Alix Barsuch
Potomac, Maryland

We had trouble with two of our young children getting out of bed. For Lauren, we found a tape called "Imagine Yourself to Sleep." For Matthew, the solution was Teddy Ruxpin, the bear who talked and told stories.

Sue Poness
Takoma Park, Maryland

Often when we said "10 more minutes before bedtime," we would end up with more negotiations for time after that 10 minutes had elapsed. So we started using a kitchen timer that we set to ring when it was bedtime. For some reason, the kids accepted the arbitrariness of the bell ringing better than our 10-minute warnings and would head off to bed without discussion.

Dee Raff
Takoma Park, Maryland

We had a bed-time ritual with John which was so soothing, and almost hypnotic for him. I would walk quietly around his room and point to the various stuffed animals and wall hangings in his room and say: "Zebra says good night... Teddy says good night... and so on." I always did this slowly and quietly. It was a wonderful ritual for both of us.

Renee Schuetter
Kailua, Hawaii

To keep your infant sleeping on her side (as is recommended by pediatricians), roll up a receiving blanket and put it behind her back in the crib or bassinet.

Brigid O'Toole
Pleasant Hill, California

When you check on your child before going to bed, hang on his bed post or crib rail a small shopping bag containing a few "good morning" toys and books, maybe even a small container of Cheerios. Always include some familiar things, like the book *Good Morning* by Helen Oxenbury. Put this special bag out of reach during the day. This might give you a few extra minutes in bed each morning.

Mary Rowley
Strongsville, Ohio

If there's construction going on in your home during baby's nap time, consider these two steps you can take to make the nursery quieter: (1) Hang a quilt or blanket over the nursery's door, and (2) Run a fan in front of the door; the white noise will help block out other sounds.

Jeff Daniels
Englewood, New Jersey

I'd been mistaking the wetness cry for the hunger cry. One night when she woke up, I tried changing Maria's diaper but not feeding her. Amazingly, she went right back to sleep! After that we looked for a diaper that would keep her drier at night. Although we still use cloth diapers during the day (because we try to do our bit for the environment), at night we use Huggies Thick disposables because they're the most absorbent diapers we've found.

Lucy Penzalos
Lexington, Kentucky

I never let Nicole nap after 4 P.M. I used to have all kinds of trouble getting her to go to sleep at a reasonable hour at night. Her pediatrician asked me how many hours a day she napped. It was sometimes more than four or five hours. He said the reason she didn't want to sleep at night was that she was getting too much sleep in the daytime. So now—though it sometimes seems crazy to me to wake a happily sleeping baby—I always get her up no more than three hours after she goes down. Then by 8 or 9 P.M. she usually feels sleepy again.

Diane Hare
Brooklyn, New York

I can't believe this worked, but when Bridget left her crib for a big bed, I told her she couldn't get out of the bed until she had my permission. She asked my permission to get out of bed in the morning for years!

Anne O'Brien
Sandusky, Ohio

When Robert was about three years old, he was ready to give up his naps, but I was not ready for that. So after lunch on weekdays, I would give him a nice, warm bath. Then we would lay on his bed reading for a short time. He always ended up taking a good nap whenever we did this.

Linda Wilhelm
Takoma Park, Maryland

Strollers

Pushing a stroller is a lot easier than carrying the baby around, though it's not as easy as having a Sherpa around. But which stroller is best? And how do you make a good one even better? Read on and heed the advice from these parents.

For the child who's always insisting on being carried rather than riding in the stroller, don't ever say, "No, I won't carry you." That keeps reminding her of the carrying option. Give your child a positive choice. Say, "You can ride in the stroller or you can hold my hand and walk with me. Which do you want?"

April Masterson
Tulsa, Oklahoma

Keep in your stroller bag:
• an extra set of house and/or car keys
• a hat for baby in case it's sunny or chilly
• a travel pack of tissues
• a small tube of baby sunscreen lotion
• an extra diaper
• a few Wash 'n Dry packs for wiping hands or washing faces
• a $10 or $20 bill and some change for making phone calls

Louise McBurney
McLean, Virginia

Make a rule from the beginning that you will not let your toddler push his or her own stroller—ever. Otherwise, every time you go anywhere, you'll have a struggle over who gets to push the stroller, you or the kid. I finally learned this with my third child!

Kathy Ladd
St. Louis, Missouri

We used a harness to keep our active child in the stroller, otherwise he would always try to climb out.

Anne O'Brien
Sandusky, Ohio

Even the lightest umbrella stroller can haul your shopping if you equip it with carrying bags. There are roomy mesh bags that attach to the back frame with clips, side-hanging bags that won't cause the stroller to tip backward when loaded, and webbed bags that attach to the handles with Velcro or are suspended lengthwise underneath the stroller as extra carrying space. When all possible carrying devices are added, you can really tote a lot of stuff.

Peggy Robin
Washington, D.C.

We have a light little umbrella stroller, but it doesn't have a sunshade. No problem. I was in a store that sold lawn furniture and found lots of small, clamp-on umbrellas that attach to the backs of chairs. I bought one for $3.99. Not only does it bend to block the sun from any angle, but it is also the same color blue as the fabric stroller seat.

Carol Rice
Wheaton, Maryland

I got tired of people asking me, "Is it a boy or a girl?" So I got a name license plate, attached it to the stroller, and now I don't have to answer the same question from strangers over and over again.

Julie Anderson
Chicago, Illinois

Before you buy a stroller, consider whether you're going to be using it mainly around the neighborhood, or if you'll be taking it with you in the car and unfolding it for use wherever you go. If it's for the former purpose, then buy the biggest stroller you can comfortably push up the hills in your neighborhood. If it's for the latter, then get one that collapses. One-touch collapsible strollers are the best.

Jane Newman
Woodstock, Vermont

Some people think it's excessive, but we have four strollers for our one baby, and we use all four of them. We bought one heavy-duty stroller for daily outings around the neighborhood. It comes with a big basket that can hold a regular-size shopping bag. We bought a light umbrella stroller that we leave in the trunk of the car, so we never have to worry about remembering to take the stroller when we go on a car trip. Then we have this very nifty though somewhat gimmicky stroller that we use for certain special outings. It folds up and converts to a backpack-carrier. We saw it in Right Start, a specialized baby products catalog. Though it's a little cumbersome for everyday use, it's perfect for when you go someplace where you'll have to cover a lot of rough ground or stairs. And the fourth stroller we leave at Grandma and Grandpa's.

Joanne Brennan
Charlottesville, Virginia

Tantrums

If your child is screaming uncontrollably, keep in mind that tantrums always end. In the meantime, may we suggest a pair of comfortable headphones? If your toddler's tantrums are driving you crazy, remember that adults yell and scream a lot, too. Read on to learn how some parents have dealt with tantrums.

Put yourself in your child's place to figure out what the tantrum is really about. Is your child feeling ignored? Is he overly tired? Does he want something that really is reasonable? For example, if your child screams when his raincoat is put on, maybe it's because the raincoat is too small or hot to wear. Once you've got a clue to the cause of the tantrum you may be closer to a solution.

Nancy Green
Boston, Massachusetts

A little bribery never hurt anyone.

Various parents

If a child is crying or having a tantrum because he wants something, don't reinforce that behavior by giving the child what he wants every time. You'll end up having a crying, whining child.

Marty Gregg
Webster Groves, Missouri

If you're in a public place and can't get the child home quickly, try picking her up and whirling her around. Making whirling sounds helps, too!

Peggy Robin
Washington, D.C.

We used charts and stars to reward good behavior whether it involved toilet training, controlling temper tantrums, or just getting through the day without major problems. Often, the children would be rewarded with something after accumulating a certain number of stars, but we found that just putting the star on the chart was usually enough reward.

Mel and Dee Raff
Takoma Park, Maryland

What a child wants is your *undivided* attention. Whenever possible I tried to give my cranky child total attention, even if for only 30 seconds: a hug, a sentence that shows I'm aware of what his situation is—but no cheating, since children know when you're holding back even a little.

Liz Malone
Silver Spring, Maryland

I learned this from a neighbor down the street. It is very useful to give notice to a child before it's time to do something: eat meals, go to bed, leave the house. With 10 minutes' warning, the child won't be surprised—or throw a tantrum—when his play is interrupted.

Rob Platky
Takoma Park, Maryland

Matthew would bang his head on the floor or the wall when he was having a tantrum. It completely unnerved me and he would end up with bumps on his forehead. My pediatrician told me not to try to stop him when he did this but to simply walk out of the room. It was hard to walk away, but I did and the behavior stopped.

Jo Mannies
Webster Groves, Missouri

My husband and I made an agreement that whenever one of us was having a confrontation with one of our daughters, the other would fade back and not enter the argument. That way, there were not two huge people against one tiny one.

Barb Schiller
St. Louis, Missouri

Recognize that a lot of carrying on in public places is the result of overstimulation. Your child just can't handle the bustle and noise of a shopping mall with so many new sights and sounds to take in. The best thing to do is to take the child outside in the fresh air as soon as possible, or at the very least to a quiet spot to let the child cool off.

Mary Jones
Vienna, Virginia

Tantrums that occur regularly at certain times, such as when your child is about to be put down for a nap or has to go to bed at night, may suggest that the child's schedule is not suited to his needs. Each child is different, so what worked for the first child may not work with the second or third. Try rearranging the schedule, moving nap time back an hour, or—*shudder*—eliminating naps. Change mealtimes around, too, if that's when the tantrums come.

Randy Gitner
Miami, Florida

Speak firmly but not angrily to your child, saying, "If you tell me calmly what you want, then we'll see what we can do to take care of it for you." Note that you're not actually promising to give the child what he wants. But the child will miss the subtlety and be satisfied that he's *won*, and you can probably provide some version of what he's demanding, creating a partial victory for both parent and child: a win-win situation.

Doris Stone
New Haven, Connecticut

Consider what the tantrum is about. Is your child yelling for a new toy in a store? Say, "You might get that toy, but it won't be today. If you really want it you'll have to calm down and wait patiently." Then, if he still remembers it a day or so later get it for him as a reward, teaching that patience pays.

Gladys Spiegalman
New York, New York

As your child's voice grows louder and more insistent, you should start speaking more softly, dropping to a whisper. Most children tend to reduce their volume to match their parents' tone.

Steve Schwartz
Brooklyn, New York

Make your time out age appropriate: two minutes for a two-year-old, three minutes for a three-year-old... Also, don't have time out in a place that is reinforcing to a child or that the child wants to go to.

Martha Dolan
Maplewood, Missouri

If your child is screaming and yelling, say, "I can't understand you when you talk so loud (or so fast). Would you please talk softer (or slower)?"

Harlan Jones
Englewood, New Jersey

Teething

Teething hurts both you and your baby. Fortunately, there are plenty of remedies. Read on and you'll see that there's no reason for your child to suffer from teething pain.

Refrigerated teething rings are fine, but why not give your baby a nutritious treat while she chomps to relieve her sore gums? I give my daughter cold, barely ripe slices of honeydew melon or peach, or freeze a banana and let her munch on that. One safety note: I make sure the pieces are either too small to choke on, or so big that she can't swallow the piece whole. And I don't let her toddle around while munching on her teething fruit.

Kate Harvey
Scottsdale, Arizona

All I can say is have Orajel or some other tooth anesthetic handy, at home, in your diaper bag, everywhere. It works when nothing else will.

Bill Adler, Jr.
Washington, D.C.

When the boys were teething, I would often give them fruit juice popsicles—homemade or store-bought. They always helped.

Marcia Wilson
Washington, D.C.

My girls had a terrible time with teething. It got so bad that I asked my dentist for some of the fruit-flavored topical gel she uses before administering shots. My pediatrician said it was okay to rub some on their gums. It helped.

Mary Rand
New Orleans, Louisiana

I use the following recipe from a natural foods cookbook to make teething biscuits. I like knowing what ingredients are in them.

> 2 tablespoons honey
> 2 tablespoons molasses
> 2 tablespoons vegetable oil
> 1 egg yolk, beaten
> 1 teaspoon pure vanilla extract
> 1/4 teaspoon salt
> 1 tablespoon soy flour
> 1 scant cup whole-wheat flour
> 1 tablespoon wheat germ

Blend the first four items and then stir in the remaining ingredients. Dough should be stiff. If it is too thick, add a little milk. Roll the dough out to 1/4-inch thickness and cut into 1-by-1½-inch strips. Put strips on an ungreased cookie sheet and bake at 350 degrees for about 15 to 20 minutes.

Kathleen Winters
Tempe, Arizona

Try frozen mini-bagels for teething babies.

Various parents

Try frozen vegetable bags.

Susan Robinson
St. Louis, Missouri

I would often put water in some bottle nipples and freeze them. When my baby was having a tough time with his teething, I would give him a frozen nipple to gnaw on—it helped with the teething pain, and the baby also got a drink of water!

Dot Starek
Hillsboro, Missouri

Our baby loves those Bavarian pretzels—the big, hard ones—when he is teething. It takes him a while to break them apart and, by that time, they are pretty well gummed down.

Grace Schiller
St. Louis, Missouri

Sucking on a bottle can often irritate a baby who is teething; it's better to give him a cup with icy water to sip from.

Judy Mosley
Affton, Missouri

To make teething gel work better, first blot the baby's gums dry with a piece of gauze or a clean washcloth. Saliva on the gums interferes with the gel's maximum effectiveness.

Debbie Allen
Takoma Park, Maryland

A cold, wet washcloth to chew on works wonders. It's better than a refrigerated teething ring.

Kathy Justice
Long Beach, California

Toilet Training

When your little one is still in diapers and has to "go," it's no problem. But consider this: Once toilet training has been accomplished and you're packed into the car and stuck in a traffic jam on the interstate—well, every parent has been there before, as you'll see in this chapter.

Don't attempt to train your child on an adult toilet. Toddlers are often nervous when their feet are dangling over the floor. Sitting over a big hole with water below is hardly reassuring either. So use a potty chair on the floor.

Stan Martin
Denver, Colorado

When traveling with a child who's not yet 100 percent trained, it's a good idea to keep a small emergency potty in the trunk of the car for those times when he suddenly announces he's "got to go" and you're not sure you'll be able to reach a bathroom in time.

Connie Frank
Chicago, Illinois

Tell your baby that the potty belongs to him. He'll feel more confident about using it if he knows that the potty is his.

Katherine Delgado
Teaneck, New Jersey

Never let your child figure out that you have any investment in this process.

Cathy Johnson
Silver Spring, Maryland

Disposable pull-up training pants make the transition period so much easier. When your toddler has an accident you can pull the pants apart like a diaper and change her. Best of all, you won't find yourself getting annoyed at the mess or the ruined clothes. This means you won't communicate any negative feelings to your toddler when she makes a "mistake."

Jane Good
Newark, New Jersey

We used those pull-up training pants for Michael, but frankly I think they prolonged the process. They are almost as absorbent as diapers, and the child can't really feel the difference between a wet diaper and wet training pants. I think we'll try something different on Mary.

Mary Pat Hennicke
St. Louis, Missouri

Don't start until the child shows some interest. The average age for toilet training seems to be around two and a half years.

Various parents

When toilet training, it helps to use underwear with pictures or cartoon characters on them which are especially appealing to the child. After all, who wants to pee on Batman or the Little Mermaid?

Emily van Loon
Takoma Park, Maryland

I don't know if this is peculiar, but when it was time for toilet training, many families just let the child run around naked for a week or so. A small child is used to going to the bathroom in his diapers, but he is more inhibited from doing it when he is naked. Obviously, this will only work if you live in a warm-weather climate or are toilet training during the summer. But it worked with Andrew!

Mary Anne Hess
Silver Spring, Maryland

Part of the problem with Ethan was getting him to sit still long enough to use the potty chair. We kept a special book next to the potty chair and read that (a lot!) when toilet training him.

Gwen Strike
Washington, D.C.

Do yourself a favor and do not compare your child's toilet-training efforts with any other child's, whether it's your sister's child or your neighbor's. Your child will eventually get the hang of it, and piling guilt on yourself for not making it happen "faster" or "better" doesn't help anyone.

Kathy Ladd
St. Louis, Missouri

We have four boys and when toilet training, my husband encouraged each of them to "make bubbles." He turned it into a game for them.

Linda Wilhelm
Washington, D.C.

When training boys, throw a handful of Cheerios in the toilet and let them try to sink them. The Cheerios float, and boys love to aim and shoot.

Deven Kurzweil
Silver Spring, Maryland

When training boys, check out the biodegradable "targets" available from the Perfectly Safe baby products catalog. They're called Tinkle Time Targets and cost about $4 for 45 or about $10 for 135.

Marcie Atkins
Philadelphia,
Pennsylvania

Put girls in dresses—with or without panties—when toilet training; it makes the mad rush to the potty chair easier when they can just lift up their dresses.

Barb Schiller
St. Louis, Missouri

We were getting nowhere with Kevin on toilet training. Part of the problem seemed to be that by the time he realized he had to go, it was too late. So we took a hint from Dr. Spock and devoted an entire day to the effort. I left his clothes off for the whole day and took the potty chair with us from room to room. It worked!

Rose Krasnow
Rockville, Maryland

Keep the potty chair in the kitchen or any room where you spend the bulk of your time. Most children don't realize until the last minute that they need to go, and having the potty in a central location rather than an upstairs bathroom makes for fewer accidents.

Brigid O'Toole
Pleasant Hill, California

We decided to wait until Andrew wanted to be toilet trained before we put him in training pants. We explained the process to him and led him through it several times, then waited. But when he finally showed interest at 2 years, 10 months, we wanted to respond immediately. Unfortunately, we had planned several activities that entailed our being away from home for most of the day. What to do? We took along a jar for Andrew to urinate in, and this proved to be a good solution. No frantic searches for gas stations or public restrooms, no rushing across a park, no accidents. He was toilet trained in a week.

Liz Malone
Silver Spring, Maryland

We let both our children follow our example. When they were each about one and a half years old, we started talking about "when you are ready." We set up a potty seat in the bathroom and explained that this was the toddler's potty seat because the big one was really big. We praised only positive results and ignored all comments about "never taking off my diaper." This was a fairly slow process, but my daughter was completely trained by two and a half years and my son by three.

Gresham Lowe
Takoma Park, Maryland

Bribe them with M & M's.

Various parents

When your baby starts announcing "poop" or "wet diaper" or something similar, it's time.

Ann Lucy
Denver, Colorado

Toys, Games, and Activities

The truth is, babies need no toys. (Does anybody's one-month-old really play with those plastic keys?) And toddlers really need very few. (Take away a half dozen of your child's stuffed animals and she probably won't even notice.) But that doesn't stop parents from acquiring lots of objects for their kids. Why not? After all, if you have only one childhood to live, it's best to live it with a lot of fun toys. Here are suggestions as to how kids—and parents—can make the most of their playtime.

Balls of all sizes and shapes—except those small enough to be swallowed—are the best baby toys. A 99¢ inflatable ball will provide fun for months. Rubber balls with lots of bounce are also a treat for any toddler.

Peggy Robin
Washington, D.C.

When you're working in the kitchen and your child is underfoot, put him on a stool or chair at the sink and let him play with a small tub of water. Put a few soap suds in and give him an eggbeater, a sponge to "wash" with, and a few empty plastic food containers—he'll stay entertained for some time.

Betsy Siebert
Lenexa, Kansas

Try Hap Palmer's "Baby Songs" video. It's nearly guaranteed to make any toddler happy.

Joyce Carroll
Brooklyn, New York

My toddler, Zachary, has long been fascinated with my home computer, especially the keyboard. Of course I keep it off limits except when Zach is sitting on my lap in my desk chair, under my complete control. At other times I keep a dust cover over the equipment that unlocks with a key. But sometimes I invite Zach to run a program with me. I have one designed especially for kids his age. I put the disk in the machine and then let him "type" like a grownup. He presses keys at random, and each key calls up a different picture on the computer screen. When he hits the E key, for example, he gets a picture of an elephant that waves its trunk and balances on a ball. I read him the caption at the bottom of the screen that says "E is for Elephant." If he strikes the C he gets a juggling clown; if he hits the M he gets a monkey swinging on a vine, and so on. To him computers are more than user-friendly, they're loads of fun.

Ian Marks
Silver Spring, Maryland

Don't spend hard-earned money on toys. We shop garage sales, accept all hand-me-downs, use the library for books, and recycle household items into toys—empty shampoo bottles make great bath toys, old dresses and purses go into a "dress-up" box, laundry powder scoopers go into the sand box, and so on.

Maggie Keely Foley
Kirkwood, Missouri

Put some toys away in the closet every few months and take them out whenever your child seems bored. They'll seem like new toys each time.

Cynthia Green
Kingston, New York

I strongly suggest *not* introducing your toddler to the fun of being swung in a laundry basket. Once a baby has been treated to this, she'll never give up the sport—at least not until your back gives out.

Bill Adler, Jr.
Washington, D.C.

Magnets on the refrigerator are a great hit, particularly when kids want to be with their parents while meals are being prepared. The alphabet and number magnets are very popular. Just be sure you buy only magnets that are too big to be swallowed.

Various parents

This was one of my kids' all-time favorite toys: I took a large cardboard box and inserted paper-towel tubes and wide wrapping-paper tubes through the sides of the box at various angles. My toddlers loved dropping things into one end of a tube and seeing where the items came out on the other side.

Mary Riley
Alexandria, Virginia

One of our best infant toys was one of those inexpensive, inflatable tubes that the baby can push away and have roll back toward him. Or you can lay the baby on top of the tube and roll him back and forth. Precrawlers especially seem to enjoy the motion, and it gets them into the crawling mode.

Mary Rowley
Strongsville, Ohio

We use the following as a reward for good behavior: Make a paper chain and have the children tear off a link every morning. The day the chain ends, plan a "mystery tour." The children have no idea where they are going. Everyone gets in the car and the fun begins.

On one of our "mystery tours," we started at the library and read books about planes, tractors, and trains. Our second stop was a local airport, where the children were allowed to get into a small aircraft. Our third stop was a tractor company, where the children got inside three tractor cabs. Our fourth stop was the local hobby shop, where they got to play with a Brio train set and watch model trains run. All three of our children, ages four, five, and six, thoroughly enjoy our mystery tours.

Rosemary Queathem
Manchester, Missouri

I bought a bunch of inexpensive paint brushes (one or two inches wide) from the hardware store, and I keep a bunch of empty orange juice cans on hand. When the kids are bored or restless, I get the brushes out and let the kids go outside and paint anything they want—with water. They will literally spend hours painting the house, the fence, the swing set...

> *Marcia Wilson*
> *Washington, D.C.*

During the warm weather, I take my baby's little bath outside and let her fill it up with hose water and play. This is a wonderful way for both of us to unwind when we get home from work and day care.

> *Marcie Atkins*
> *Philadelphia,*
> *Pennsylvania*

Try box sledding. Put your toddler in any old box and push him around on the rug. Lots of fun for everyone.

> *Bill Adler, Jr., and*
> *Peggy Robin*
> *Washington, D.C.*

Don't throw away your end-of-the-year picture calendars. Give them to your toddler, who will love the pictures, especially if it's an animal calendar.

> *Rich Kaplan*
> *New York, New York*

Let your child have a steady stream of art material. Teacher supply stores are a great place to find good arts-and-crafts supplies. Also, be sure you have a place to store things like old wrapping paper, Styrofoam meat trays, buttons, berry baskets, toilet-paper tubes, yarn, and so forth.

> *Various parents*

Instead of buying a fancy toy to hang over the crib for an infant's entertainment, tie a bunch of household items to a piece of string and suspend that over the crib. We tied some old-fashioned metal measuring spoons, some bells, and a few colorful items on a string and let Elinor bat at them. Of course we made sure that the string is secured at both ends and is up so high that the baby cannot grab it, pull it down, or get her hands caught in it. This crib-hanging toy is great for the first few months, but as soon as the baby is able to sit up or prop herself up on her own, it's time to take it down.

Carol Mermey
San Francisco,
California

Here's a way to turn your junk mail into a baby toy: Kathy, our 18-month-old, loves to play with envelopes with clear plastic windows. The bigger the envelope, the better. These envelopes provide a wonderful distraction at the changing table.

Dorothy Wills
Newcastle, Delaware

One of our favorite winter activities is to "camp" in our living room. We set up the girls' little tent (a sheet over a few chairs will work just fine), make a fire in the fireplace, and pretend we are outdoors. They love it.

Patty Bohn
Webster Groves, Missouri

Here's a quick recipe for play dough. Mix four cups of flour with one and a half cups of salt. Slowly add two cups of water and one tablespoon of vegetable oil. Knead until smooth and pliable. A few drops of food coloring will make your play dough green, yellow, blue, or pink. Want to save your child's creations? Just leave them out in the sun for a few hours to harden. Then paint with bright, nontoxic colors.

Cindy Gleason
Charlottesville, Virginia

Justin loves to throw his toys on the floor and watch me pick them up. I got tired of playing the role of Human Retriever. Here's my advice on how to solve this problem:

Look in your toy store for plastic links that come in many different shapes: ovals, stars, fishes. They are very baby-safe and too large to be swallowed. Make them into a chain to attach toys to the side of a stroller, bouncer seat, crib, or playpen. Justin just loves to push his rattle off the tray of his high chair and use the chain of links to reel the toy back in.

Deena Jensen
Bethesda, Maryland

A set of plastic food-storage bowls or measuring cups that fit inside one another are just as good for a toddler as any of those "scientifically designed" nesting or stacking sets that child-development books say toddlers need. They're a lot cheaper, too, and when your toddler is done with them you can wash them off and use them in the kitchen!

Louise Lansky
Minneapolis, Minnesota

Just a warning: If you give your toddler a battery-operated cat, dog, or other animal, she's going to insist that it be turned on whenever the toy is in view. This is okay if you can stand a yapping puppy for hours on end.

Lucy Martin
Bethesda, Maryland

I tend to buy only those toys I've seen other kids enjoying at the playground near me. That way I can tell if a toy is good for just a few minutes or is something I see the kid going back to and enjoying day after day. I save a lot of money and aggravation because I'm only buying those toys I'm reasonably sure my own child will actually like.

Toni Walls
New York, New York

When Janet first started experimenting with sounds and words, one thing she enjoyed a lot was a rhyming game I made up. Whenever she used a certain word or phrase, I asked her a question to which the answer was a rhyming word or phrase. For example, if she said, "We go to park," I'd say, "Dogs go...?" and she'd answer "bark." I always stuck to the same rhyming word each time, so park was always paired with bark, shoe rhymed with blue, Janet rhymed with planet, and noisy was always paired with "a town in Idaho (Boise)." Many years later when Janet was in school and had to learn all the state capitals, there was one she had no trouble remembering, having known it since she was two.

Andrea Spence
Leesburg, Virginia

Let me tell you from experience: There's no worse crisis in a young child's life than to lose a favorite stuffed animal or doll. Tina had a Raggedy Ann doll that slept in her crib with her every night. She loved it so much that we even packed it and took it along with us on vacation. But then disaster struck. We went on a boat ride and the wind was blowing, and Raggedy Ann was swept overboard. Tina was devastated. Fortunately I knew we'd be able to buy an identical Raggedy Ann at a toy store, so I told her, "Don't worry. Tomorrow I'll bring Raggedy Ann to you, looking better than ever." What I learned from that episode is, if you think your child is developing a strong attachment to any object—a toy, a blanket—buy a spare one to keep in reserve. When the crisis hits, as it inevitably will, you won't have to go scrambling to find a replacement.

Melissa Scripps
Oswego, New York

Here are some good, free toys for a six- to nine-month-old: empty Kleenex boxes, pie pans, old cotton or silk handkerchiefs, empty video- or tape-cassette boxes, and plastic tumblers.

Gail Zucker
Los Angeles, California

Ricky has a lot of books, but his very favorite is the one I made for him.
I bought a smallish photo album, the kind with white cardboard pages
overlaid with a clear plastic film that can be peeled back, allowing you
to fit photos of any size onto each page. Of course you can insert a lot
more than photos in the book. I put in pictures of other babies I had
clipped from magazines, and drawings that I had done myself, Ricky's
scribbles, and postcards his grandparents had sent him from their
vacation. I labeled each page with a caption written with a big, brightly
colored marking pen. Because each page is covered with the plastic
film, there's no worry that the baby will be able to lick off the ink, and
because the pages are so thick, he can turn them himself without
giving himself a paper cut.

Mary Ellen McDougall
Sarasota, Florida

Want your kids to spend less time in front of the TV on Saturday
mornings? Take them for a nature walk. It doesn't have to be to a
faraway forest. You can point out all the interesting animals and plants
you find in the few blocks around your home. Look up in the trees to
see squirrel nests and under rocks for earthworms and insects. Point
out the different types of birds, flowers, shrubs—whatever you find
along the way. For children under three, identify things simply: pretty
flower, big dog, red-leafed tree. For kids four and up, take along a field
guide with big colorful pictures and let them match the pictures in the
book with the things they see in nature.

Susan Wellner
Phoenix, Arizona

It's very tempting to park your kids in front of the VCR and put on a
children's movie when they become old enough to follow a story and can
sit for an hour or so. But be warned, not all the "children's classics" are
really suitable for young children. We've learned that *Bambi* can be
terrifying to a two-year-old. *Beauty and the Beast* is too scary for our
three-year-old, and so is *101 Dalmatians*. I vividly remember being
scared out of my wits by the witch in *The Wizard of Oz* at age five. It's
usually a good idea to ask parents of slightly older children what their
kids enjoyed when they were the same age as yours. These choices are
usually safe: D-TV (those Disney animated music videos), Winnie the
Pooh half-hour stories, and all the Sesame Street videos.

Claire Schoenfeld
Greenbelt, Maryland

The "toy" Jonathan seemed to covet most was the remote control to our TV set, but of course we didn't want him to slobber all over it. We found him the perfect substitute: One of our old hand-held calculators with the batteries removed. It's the same size and color as the remote, it has just as many interesting buttons, and it tastes the same—but he can't change the channels on us while we're watching a show.

Diane Robinson
Ann Arbor, Michigan

Here's a mobile that my baby liked as much as those expensive, "scientifically designed" infant stimulation mobiles they sell in the baby catalogs. Get four or five sturdy white paper plates—the dessert-size Chinet brand works well. Using blue, green, red, and purple wide-tipped marking pens, draw simple smiling faces on one side of the plates. On the other side use a thick-tipped black marker to make interesting black-and-white patterns. Use a large embroidery hoop and nylon thread or string to hang the plates. Put a hook in the ceiling and hang the mobile from it, but be sure to take it down when the baby's old enough to reach out and grab those swirling plates.

Ellen Saddleman
Cleveland, Ohio

A good toy for a baby who's exploring new sensations: Start with a large, thick cotton gardening glove. Get seven patches of leftover fabric in different, interesting textures, colors, and patterns: satin, corduroy, velvet, seersucker, lace, terry cloth, stripes, dots, flowered patterns. Sew a different piece around each finger end and one big piece on the palm and another on the back of the glove. Put a bell inside the glove, sew it shut, and *voilà!*

Flora Shulman
Bethesda, Maryland

Plastic Easter eggs are one of the best toys going!

Various parents

Kelley loves to hear songs from Broadway shows because she thinks they're all about her. I sing "Hello, Kelley" to the tune of "Hello, Dolly." I sing "Don't Cry for Me, Kelley Robbins" from *Evita* whenever she's fussy. I sing "Kelley Robbins, You're OK!" to the title tune from *Oklahoma!* and change all the lyrics to describe whatever we're doing. One day I'll have to break it to her that her mommy didn't write all these wonderful tunes.

Marianne Robbins
Boston, Massachusetts

Just as it's easier for children to learn the alphabet by singing it, it's easier for them to learn to count when they learn the numbers as part of a rhyme. I taught my child "One, two, buckle my shoe," and he could count to 10 before he was two. He also learned "2, 4, 6, 8, who do we appreciate?" and that taught him how to count by 2's.

Shelby Seidner
Pittsburgh, Pennsylvania

Start telling your child early and often that television commercials are just made-up stories and are (almost) never true. Say, "That doll doesn't really do all those things—it's just a trick of the camera that makes it look that way." Instill this skepticism early, and your child will end up more satisfied with the toys that you do buy and less likely to demand the toys you refuse to buy.

Peggy Blau
Kingston, New York

Try a harmonica. For just about any toddler over the age of one, it's the perfect toy. They blow out, it plays a note. They breathe in, it plays another note.

Bill Adler, Jr.
Washington, D.C.

Never let your toddler see an "adult toy"—a Nintendo Gameboy or a TV remote control, for example—that you don't intend for him to be able to play with.

Susan Dupre
Lexington, Kentucky

Travel and Vacations

When traveling with a toddler, the first thing you have to understand is that it's not going to be a real vacation, not like when you and your spouse were dating or were on your honeymoon. One thing's for sure— taking a vacation with your kids will make you appreciate your parents a lot more. When vacationing with a child you can either travel heavy or very heavy. Bill's sister went away with her six-month-old one summer. She and her husband, Shawn, did the trip in two segments: Trip one—Shawn went up to the rental house with a rental station wagon containing everything they would need for the first two days. Trip two—the rest of the stuff, Mom, and the baby went up in their car. With all the extra work that's involved in traveling with a pint-sized human, why bother to go at all? Because it's fun; as you'll see from the stories and experiences in this chapter.

If you'll be staying at a hotel or motel, don't bother to pack a lot of bibs. Use a hotel washcloth or napkin to protect your baby's clothes, hanging it around the baby's neck with a bib clip. That's an inexpensive little item you can find in many variety stores or baby catalogs, or you can make one yourself with two small plastic clothespins connected by a short piece of satin or grosgrain ribbon.

Anne Dickson
Atlanta, Georgia

Buy each child a scrapbook and let him keep it up-to-date during the whole trip. Things to go in the scrapbook: soap wrappers from hotels, sugar wrappers from restaurants, free postcards from the hotel rooms, brochures. Your child can draw things and copy words he has seen. It always keeps our boys occupied on trips.

Sally Tippett Rains
St. Louis, Missouri

When using hotel cribs, place a blanket *under* the crib mattress and bring the sides of the blanket up to form bumpers. We did this in the middle of one night when the baby kept "klunking" into the sides of the crib in a small hotel room.

> *Jan Hernon*
> *St. Louis, Missouri*

Carefully inspect the crib provided by a hotel. Not all hotel cribs are up to current safety standards, and some hotels, dangerously, provide double mattresses.

> *Hatti Gem*
> *Riverside, Kentucky*

When we didn't have crib bumpers on a hotel crib or at a friend's house, I would weave an extra bedsheet in and out of the crib railings to improvise bumpers.

> *Dot Starek*
> *Hillsboro, Missouri*

When visiting grandparents at vacation homes (or at any vacation destination that has decks or balconies), secure deck railings by wrapping fishing line cross-wise between the slats to create an invisible fence. This will not obstruct the view but will make the deck or balcony safer. The line can be removed after the baby leaves, and Grandpa can even use it for its original purpose again.

> *"Grandpa" John Amend*
> *Ballwin, Missouri*

For our children's first few years of life, an illness was inevitable every time we took a trip. We've visited pediatricians in more than a dozen cities around the country! If you're staying in a hotel and need to consult a doctor, ask the concierge for a recommendation. Many large hotels have doctors on call who will actually make house calls to your room. If that fails, ask some hotel employees to recommend their own children's doctors. Always carry over-the-counter products like acetaminophen and Pedialyte, as you're bound to need them at times when it's inconvenient to go out and buy them.

> *Martha Shirk*
> *Webster Groves, Missouri*

When going on a family vacation, it's helpful to pack an entire day's clothing (down to underwear and socks) for your child in a large zip-lock bag. It eliminates the difficulty of finding all the clothes in a packed suitcase, as well as fighting over what to wear.

Jan Paul
Webster Groves, Missouri

When you are going into a crowded place such as an amusement park, put the same bright-colored T-shirts on all the children in your group. It makes it easier to spot them if they step away.

Frances Noonan
Kirkwood, Missouri

I always pack two kinds of eardrops when we go on vacation. The first is an over-the-counter kind that helps prevent swimmer's ear, which is often picked up from hotel pools. The second is called Auralgan, also available over-the-counter; these eardrops plus Tylenol help control the pain of earaches until you can get antibiotics.

Mary Anne Hess
Silver Spring, Maryland

When we're feeding the baby on the road, we like the convenience and dependable hygiene of disposable products. You can get formula in presterilized disposable bottles called nursettes. They come in 4- or 6-ounce sizes. You just stick on a clean nipple, feed the baby, remove the nipple, and toss the bottle out. No worrying about keeping the formula chilled and having to warm it up. We also like using disposable bibs, which our local supermarket carries. They come 5 or 10 to a pack and are made of a thin, spongy material that really absorbs spills. We always keep a giant roll of paper towels in the car so that wherever we stop, we can always create a clean surface to put the baby on. With the way she spits up, if we used blankets we'd need a fresh one every hour!

Mark Richards
Albuquerque, New
Mexico

If you're going on a day-long trip and need to carry four or more bottles upright in your cooler, first put them in an empty six-pack carton before putting them in the cooler.

Alice Travian
Portland, Maine

We used to put premeasured, powdered formula in bottles to carry with us when we travel. Now that Jeffrey has graduated from formula to milk, I carry a bottle with premeasured, powdered milk, so all I have to do is add water.

Grace Olds
New Haven, Connecticut

Get a small, loose-leaf notebook with divider tabs. Before the trip, record in the notebook needed information organized city by city according to your itinerary. Include for each city:
• phone numbers of friends, hotels, and other places to stay
• information on sitters
• hospitals
• a list of good places to take children

Katherine Albert
Memphis, Tennessee

The best vacation we ever had was arranged by a travel agent who specialized in family travel. She booked us into hotels that were set up to deal with young children. They had babysitting available, good cribs, and refrigerators and microwaves for preparing baby food. The agent planned an itinerary for us that she knew from experience was within the travel tolerance of kids of a certain age, and she recommended sights and activities that our kids would like. We found her just by looking in the Yellow Pages under travel agencies and reading the ads until we hit on one that listed family travel as an area of expertise.

Robert Franke
Philadelphia,
Pennsylvania

Pack your baby's clothes in zip-lock baggies. This cuts down on the space needed in your suitcase, and the baggies are handy if the clothes become soiled.

Susan Robinson
St. Louis, Missouri

We traveled to a lot of places when Julia was very young, including Spain and Italy. We usually planned our days by starting with a good breakfast, followed by some strenuous activity and an outdoor picnic lunch. We would save our museum visits for the afternoon, when Julia's energy was expended and she was content to rest in a stroller.

Bobbie Tate
Takoma Park, Maryland

When planning a family vacation, consider your child's developmental level. Theme parks and sedate museums can be a nightmare with toddlers. Head instead to a beach.

Another alternative is to choose a hotel or resort that offers quality children's activities. That way you and your spouse will get some time off to do the things you want. Also, take turns taking care of your child, so you feel like you are getting a vacation from parenting responsibilities.

Martha Shirk
Webster Groves, Missouri

Our best vacations with the kids have been shared with another couple who have kids close to the ages of our own. That way we can trade off babysitting for each other's kids and do some adult things, leaving all the kids home with one adult to supervise. The kids like it because they have playmates along. It also cuts costs to split expenses with another couple. We've been able to get great suites in hotels together, instead of the smaller rooms we would have had to take if we'd planned separate vacations.

Marilyn Grillo
Los Angeles, California

To get down to the smallest number of bags for efficient travel, I eliminate the diaper bag. I carry a very large pocketbook with many compartments. Some are for my things and others are for changing the baby. I don't carry a large changing pad, only a thin piece of rubberized canvas that I can fold up and stash easily in my bag, and I buy wipes and tissues in small travel-size packs. Everything's very light, so I don't feel that I'm lugging around a lot of stuff, but I'm still well equipped for a change whenever necessary.

Julie Moser
Potomac, Maryland

I learned the hard way to always order the children's meal for young ones when making plane reservations. On one particularly gruesome flight, we were seated near the rear of a very big, very crowded airplane. My supply of crackers had been ravenously consumed in the terminal because of a flight delay, and my crew of kids was starving by the time the plane took off. We smelled the food a full 45 minutes before it was served to us in the back of the plane, and when it got there the kids were dismayed by the breaded tomatoes and unidentifiable meat, which was smothered in an unidentifiable sauce. On our return flight, I called the airline ahead of time and ordered children's meals for each of our three young travelers. Their meals were delivered to our seats before the other passengers were served, and the meals consisted of plain hamburgers, fruit cocktail, and milk—all identifiable and palatable to little ones.

Mary Ellen Koenig
Takoma Park, Maryland

When traveling with a baby in hot weather, keep a few rubber pacifiers in a small cooler-type jug with ice and water. When baby has finished with one, offer a fresh, new, juicy, cold pacifier. This may keep her happy during the trip.

Linda Ambroso
Arlington, Virginia

Take along a Cup of Soup container when you travel on an extended airplane trip. Practically every toddler loves noodles, and with Cup of Soup all you need is hot water to make your toddler a meal. There's always hot water available on airplanes.

Bill Adler, Jr.
Washington, D.C.

When taking a plane trip, I bring gum but don't tell my kids. Right as we begin to take off, I give them each a piece to relieve any pressure on their eardrums. As soon as we're up in the air, I make them dispose of it by promising them a surprise. The surprise is always in their backpacks—healthy snacks, games, and activities for the plane ride.

Sally Tippett Rains
St. Louis, Missouri

Take along the following on any plane or train trip:
• bottles (unless baby is nursing)
• security blanket or favorite stuffed animal
• other small toys to bring out one by one as the trip wears on
• easy, portable food you know your baby likes
• something for you to munch on

Carol Rice
Seattle, Washington

When traveling, wrap a variety of small presents for the children— things like fruit roll-ups or crayons. Dole them out on the plane as rewards for good behavior.

Various parents

The key to flying with a child under two years old is not where you're going but whether the flight is nonstop. The fewer landings and takeoffs the baby has to endure, the better.

Bill Adler, Jr.
Washington, D.C.

Limit as much as possible the number of things to carry. Fit clothing for you, your spouse, and your kids into a single, large, *wheeled* piece of luggage. Combine diaper bag and pocketbook into one carry-on bag. To avoid having to carry the baby, take along an umbrella stroller that folds up small enough to fit in the plane's overhead compartment. When you hook the carry-on bag over the stroller's handles, you end up not having to carry anything!

Peggy Robin
Washington, D.C.

Calling ahead is the key to convenient travel with kids. We call rental-car companies ahead of time to let them know we need a car safety seat. When we've called airlines ahead of time to let them know we're traveling with a baby and an older child, we've been pleasantly surprised to find them willing to help us with a variety of tasks: They always let us board the plane first and help us stow the umbrella stroller in the overhead compartment; they've warmed baby food for us and even had formula on hand when we requested it ahead of time. And while the plane sat waiting on the runway, the flight attendant let our little boy get a look at the cockpit and meet the pilot and copilot. Our kids have had as much fun on the flights as they did at our destinations.

Molly Hines
Princeton, New Jersey

Two things make flying with a baby difficult: Where do you change the baby, and how do you help the baby cope with the pressure change during takeoff and landing? Here's what works for me. I put the baby in a fresh diaper as close to boarding time as I can get. Since my baby tends to dirty his diaper just once a day, mid-morning, I try to schedule my flights for noon or later. I use a diaper of "overnight" absorbency, and if the flight is less than five hours, I just wait till we get to the other airport to make the change. If the flight involves any layovers or plane changes, I do the necessary diapering during that time. To distract him from the uncomfortable feeling in his ears during takeoffs and landings, I always give him a bottle of apple juice (before he was weaned, I always nursed him during takeoffs and landings). Flying cross-country with a baby is still not a pleasure, but it sure beats driving with him for a week.

Penny Remnick
Newton, Massachusetts

The easiest way to take a long car trip with a baby is to travel at night, past the baby's bedtime. Sarah consistently falls asleep at 9 P.M. and stays sound asleep whether she's in her crib or in her car seat, until hunger wakes her. On one trip we got six hours of driving behind us before she woke up. And the roads are less crowded at night, so driving is less stressful.

Catherine Alessio
Burlington, Vermont

When traveling with small children I take along a box of gallon-size plastic storage bags. They're useful for so many things. I can use them as garbage bags for dirty diapers and other trash; I can use them as small laundry bags for dirty clothes, or keep the kids' wet swimsuits in them; I can keep treats in them to dole out in small amounts during the trip; I use them as containers for toys, games, and art supplies for the road; I can keep their toothbrushes and bottle nipples clean and separate from their other luggage. I've hardly begun to discover all the possible uses of the plastic storage bag.

Shelley Kramer
Columbia, Maryland

Music is the key for a fun trip with our kids. We have a cassette player in the car, and we always make sure to bring the kids' favorite tapes. They like to sing along or supply the responses to songs that call for the child to fill in his name or answer other questions. Read-aloud tapes are also good for a few hours. I've even made my own read-aloud tapes, choosing books with several chapters and some gentle suspense, so that the kids don't want to stop until they find out what happens to the characters in the end.

Dwayne Howard
Denver, Colorado

About the Authors

Bill Adler, Jr., is president of Adler & Robin Books, Inc., a literary agency and book packaging firm. Adler & Robin Books represents a wide range of nonfiction books for adults. Adler is past president of Washington Independent Writers, the country's largest regional writers' organization. He is the author of more than half a dozen books including *Outwitting Squirrels* (Chicago Review Press, 1988), *The Non-Smoker's Bill of Rights* (William Morrow, 1989), *The Home Remodeler's Combat Manual* (HarperCollins, 1991), *Outwitting Critters* (HarperCollins, 1992), and *Impeccable Birdfeeding* (Chicago Review Press, 1992). He and his daughter, Karen, coauthored *An English-Baby, Baby-English Dictionary: A Dictionary for Parents and Infants* (Pocket Books, 1993).

He received a B.A. from Wesleyan University, where he majored in government and did graduate work in organic chemistry. He received an M.A. from Columbia University's School of International Affairs, specializing in Soviet foreign policy.

Peggy Robin is vice president of Adler & Robin Books, Inc. She received a B.A. from the University of California at Berkeley. Robin is the author of *Saving the Neighborhood: You Can Fight Developers and Win!* (Woodbine House, 1990) and *How to Be a Successful Fertility Patient* (William Morrow, 1993). Her articles have appeared in *The Washington Post* and other publications.